BRING OUT THE *Millionaire* IN YOU

YOUR JOURNEY TO **FINANCIAL FREEDOM**

Free Bonuses
Bring
OutThe
Millionaire
.com

Angela Dees

AWARD WINNING AUTHOR

Foreword by Raymond Aaron
New York Times Bestselling Author

Bring Out The Millionaire In You: Your Journey To Financial Freedom
www.bringoutthemillionaire.com
Copyright © 2017 Angela Dees

ISBN-13: 978-1973778721

Publisher
10-10-10 Publishing
Markham, ON
Canada

Printed in Canada and the United States of America

THE JOURNEY

FOREWORD

Are you interested in becoming a millionaire? Then, this book is for you. I am so proud to introduce this book, *Bring Out The Millionaire In You* by author Angela Dees as it provides a simple and easy-to-use blueprint for you to use on your journey to financial freedom.

Angela begins by first helping you to develop a millionaire's mindset, which is necessary for you to enjoy the journey as you travel the different roads to financial freedom. Then she guides you through the different streets on the journey—Stewardship Street, Budget Boardwalk, Debt-Free Drive, to name a few. On each part of the journey, she shares simple, easy-to-understand financial strategies and biblical principles that you can begin using today to bring out the millionaire in you.

This is not your average financial textbook. Angela challenges you to personalize your journey and do the work necessary to create the life you desire. Her conversational and sometimes humorous style helps bring some levity to a serious and often overlooked area. She encourages, inspires, and gives you simple steps to take so that you can set some realistic goals and then take the actions to execute them. I know that you will be enriched by the lessons that you learn on each part of your journey. Read the book, do the work, and if you really want to make this journey simple, use the powerful tools and resources that she provides on her website. You will especially like Real Estate Parkway because she addresses personal home ownership and encourages you to consider real estate as a part of your overall investment portfolio. Having bought and sold over 1,100 properties in my lifetime, I can attest to the power of real estate in building wealth over the long term.

Angela's twenty plus years of experience in working with individuals in the financial services industry, and later business owners in the private sector, is evident in the ease with which she presents the information. I am so proud of the work that she has put together and I am excited for you, the reader, as you begin your personal journey to BRING OUT THE MILLIONAIRE IN YOU.

Raymond Aaron
New York Times Best Selling Author

About *Bring Out the Millionaire in You*

I feel the need to share with you how this book came about. While living in Atlanta, in the late 90s, I attended Ben Hill United Methodist Church. Having worked in the financial industry for about three years at the time, I went to the church to offer my services in free financial seminars. Instead, I stumbled upon a Bible study called Crown Ministries. This was a twelve-week class that taught biblical principles and financial strategies concerning finances. It changed my life forever.

My husband, Kevin, and I enrolled, and I really became even more excited about my role in the financial services industry because I now understood that I was helping people to implement the things that God explains we are to do financially. Things like: leaving an inheritance to your children's children through life insurance; diversifying and investing, like the story in Matthew about the parable of the talents; getting out of debt; and much more.

Kevin and I later went on to facilitate the class at least once a year for about four years. During that time, I also served as the Financial Education Team chairperson, and that is when God gave me the idea for *The Millionaire in You: Your Journey To Financial Freedom*. I told everyone it is a book in progress. I'm writing it as I live it; and, yes, it is an ongoing journey.

Fast forward to 2017; a lot has changed. I now live in Houston, TX, I am the Finance Manager for my family's business, and Kevin and I also have a real estate business. I now have real life experiences to share with you about my journey, from the perspective of a person who has had both triumphs and challenges. I can tell you some of the detours

I took and some of the things I had to do to get back on my journey to financial freedom. Where appropriate, I will also share with you stories of other people who have helped me along the journey, who share some strategies and practices that I previously did not know. I offer this glimpse into my life and that of others as encouragement for you as you go along on your journey. Maybe you have hit some similar roadblocks, or maybe you've taken some great detours that have already led to a great journey; if so, I invite you to share your success stories with me on my website, www.bringoutthemillionaire.com.

My ultimate prayer is that you will FOCUS ON YOUR JOURNEY. This journey is a personal one that only YOU can travel. It will require that YOU develop a true relationship with God; that YOU make some decisions about YOUR financial and spiritual well-being; that YOU learn to involve God in your finances and recognize that He has the power to do all that YOU think, ask, or imagine.

I am so excited for you because I know that your life will be changed for the better if YOU apply the biblical principles AND financial strategies covered in this book. It is then that YOU will "...learn to be content in whatever circumstance you are in. You will know how to get along with humble means, and know how to live in prosperity; in any and every circumstance you will have learned the secret of being filled and going hungry, both of having abundance and suffering need. You will know that you CAN do all things through Christ who strengthens you." (paraphrase of Philippians 4:11-13)

Enjoy the Journey!!!
Angela Dees

Let the Journey Begin!

Becoming a millionaire on paper is simple. Realizing you are a millionaire right now is imperative. Throughout this journey, you will travel from Stewardship Street to Millionaire's Row, where you will learn biblical principles and practical financial strategies to help you **do both**.

Now, I'm sure you may be thinking, "Look, just tell me how to become a millionaire on paper; all that spiritual stuff is not going to help me pay my bills, buy things for myself and loved ones, or help me to see the world. I need to know how to become a 'real millionaire'—and I don't want to wait until the last chapter to find out."

Relax; you will receive the simple steps to become a "real millionaire." More importantly, you will discover the true peace and contentment that comes from the realization that you are a millionaire right now. With that in mind, Let The Journey Begin!!!

Chapter 1

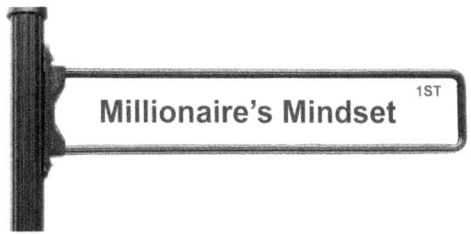

Millionaire's Mindset 1ST

Do you know who you are?

I know who I am. I'm Lee Hampton and Eva Hampton's daughter; Debbie's little sister; Kevin's wife; Kirk's mom; and Hamp's (Kelvin, Randy, or Rodney) youngest sister. I am the youngest of five siblings, and I have a rich family heritage. I come from a loving, close, crazy, laugh out loud, live life large, type of family. I have a family of entrepreneurs, teachers, and even a former professional athlete (my brother, Rodney Hampton). As the "baby" of my family, I went through life knowing that my family had my back. Even though my mom and dad divorced when I was around 12, I never wondered or worried about having food to eat, money to do things, transportation, etc. My dad always supplied what we needed, and a lot of what we wanted, both before and after the divorce. My mom worked tirelessly as a beautician to provide for the five of us and, typically, she provided food for at least one or two cousins who would often be at our house.

I tell you this because I remember being shocked when I learned in my high school economics class that we were poor! What? Why didn't someone tell me? We had a nice house, and my mom always drove a nice car. We ate well—my mom can really cook. Sure, I had to work to have a little extra money in my pocket—who didn't? However, in my high school economics class, I learned that the federal poverty level at the time was like $18,000 of income per year for a household. I remember going home to my mom and saying, "Guess what, Mom; we're poor." She laughed, because she knew I knew that we weren't poor just because some report from Washington, DC said so.

You see, even though I was technically poor, I never knew it. I was raised with a *Millionaire's Mindset.* My mom and dad taught me the value of working for what I wanted, managing the resources that I had, and striving for excellence in everything that I did. Even though neither of them had a college degree, they presented college as the path to economic freedom for me and my siblings. I have a rich family heritage because of who my parents are and because of who my siblings are. I enjoyed so much favor and privilege because every teacher at the school knew my mom. After all, Mom had always been an involved parent and there were four kids before me. If they didn't know my mom, they knew one, if not all, of my siblings. So, I enjoyed privileges just because of my relationship with my family. They spoiled me. Then, when I married my college sweetheart, Kevin Dees, he continued where they left off.

Even though I am married, I will always be a *Hampton,* because that is my father's name. I will always have access to all the privileges that come with that title and with being Lee Hampton's "baby girl." However, there is one title I have that is above that one, and that is— God's child.

It is my title as *God's child* that helps me to know that I AM ALREADY A MILLIONAIRE. Look at some definitions of millionaire; then, I will share with you why I feel that I am one already.

Millionaire on Paper Defined

Millionaire
Noun
1. A person whose wealth amounts to a million or more in some unit of currency, as dollars.
2. Any very rich person.
Millionaire. *Dictionary.com Unabridged*. Random House, Inc. 19 Jan. 2017.
<Dictionary.com http://www.dictionary.com/browse/millionaire>.

Millionaire—n. man of wealth or means, capitalist, tycoon, rich man, moneyed man, man of substance
Webster's New World Thesaurus, 1974

Millionaire—a person who has accumulated a net worth (assets minus liabilities) totaling at least 1 million dollars.
Common Definition by Financial Person

Millionaire— someone who has unlimited wealth, is rich, and whose money works for them
Common Definition by The Average Adult

Millionaire by Relationship

The preceding definitions speak to becoming a millionaire on paper. I would like to explain why I have a millionaire's mindset and consider myself to be a millionaire right now, even while I am journeying to become a millionaire on paper.

Read the following two scripture verses:

"Now I say that the heir, as long as he is a child, does not differ at all from a slave, though he is master of all, but is under guardians and stewards until the time appointed by the father. Even so, we, when we were children, were in bondage under the elements of the world. But when the fullness of the time had come, God sent forth His Son, born of a woman, born under the law, to redeem those who were under the law, that we might receive the adoption as sons."

"And because you are sons, God has sent forth the Spirit of His Son into your hearts, crying out, 'Abba, Father!' Therefore, you are no longer a slave but a son, and if a son, then an heir of God through Christ." (https://www.bible.com/bible/114/GAL.4:1-7.nkjv)

What are we heirs to?

"For every beast of the forest is Mine, and the cattle on a thousand hills. I know all the birds of the mountains, And the wild beast of the field are Mine. If I were hungry, I would not tell you, For the world is Mine, and all its fullness." (Psalm 50:10-12)

Because I am a co-heir with Christ (Galatians 4), I am a co-heir to everything God owns. (Psalm 50:10-12) You don't have to be a rocket scientist to understand the concept of inheritance. When a family member passes away, they leave a will to have their assets distributed to their loved ones, their heirs. According to Galatians 4, As a child of God, I am an heir and have rights to everything God owns.

Do the mental math for yourself. Can you put a price on the cattle on a thousand hills? How about every beast of the field? All the birds of the mountains? Wait, let's calculate the value of the entire earth and all its fullness! Now, if you are a math person and really want to get bogged down doing the calculation, go ahead. I am just trying to get you to understand that by your relationship with God, if you have one, you are already a millionaire. You just need to start acting like it. You need to develop a mindset that will help you to understand your true inheritance and the true purpose for wealth—to glorify God through our gifts to others.

Assets

Every beast of the forest	$_____
Cattle on a thousand hills	$_____
All the birds of the mountains	$_____
The world	$_____
Liabilities	$_____
Net Worth (Assets- Liabilities)	$_____

Why does it matter?

I believe when you know who you are, you carry yourself differently. When you understand how powerful and how awesome God is, you approach life and, especially, life's challenges with a more positive attitude. You walk victoriously, so problems merely become situations. These are just some of the benefits of knowing who you are.

So again, I ask: do you know who you are?

LEAVE A NOTE FOR YOUR DADDY

When I was younger, and I needed money for extra activities or other things that my mom may not have immediate cash for, she would tell me, "Leave a note for your daddy."

Whether it was $10 for a fieldtrip, $30 for some new shoes, or $500 for a spring break trip, I would leave a note or, as I got older, call my dad to put my request in. When my dad came in at night, he would read the note and leave the money for me so I could have it in the morning.

I suppose this is why I never knew we were poor. LOL!! You see, I always thought we were well off because if I ever needed something, I would just ask my daddy. Even when I just wanted something, I would just ask my daddy. No, that does not mean that my mom and dad gave us everything we ever wanted, or that we ever asked for. My mom and my sister would provide most of the money and funds that I needed for the everyday necessities; they only instructed me to leave a note or call my dad for the extras or, in my case, the *big ticket* items. I did tell you I was the baby, right? (My requests were usually not frequent, but they were BIG!)

Now, imagine how this made me feel as a child. At a young age, it was impressed upon me that if I had a need, all I had to do was leave a note for my daddy, and he would grant my request. Sometimes he would grant it right away if it was a simple request. Other times, depending on the deadline, he would take a couple of days and then take care of it. The point is, I always knew that if I made a request, it would be answered one way or the other. Most of the time, the answer was *yes*. I honestly cannot think of a good request where the answer was *no*.

This really helped me to develop a millionaire's mindset at an early age. Both of my parents always taught me that there is nothing that I cannot do if only I would be willing to work for it. This experience of leaving a note for my daddy, however, taught me that there was nothing I could not have, if only I left a note for my daddy.

So, in my eyes, my dad was rich. I knew he had to work, but he also had this vending machine business, and this was one of the ways he was able to provide some of the extras that we needed.

If my earthly father could provide most of what I requested, how much more could my heavenly father provide? I want to encourage you to *leave your Daddy a note.*

Let Him Know what you need. He is interested in knowing what you need. He clearly says, in Luke 11:13, "If you then, though you are evil, know how to give good gifts to your children, how much more will your Father in heaven give the Holy Spirit to those who ask him?"

Move your ASSets!!

I remember when my oldest brother was in high school, and during the summer my mom required all of us to work. Well, he had worked one or two jobs that summer that did not pan out. I think he was on an ice cream truck for a couple of days ringing the bell and selling ice cream. Then he fried chicken at a fast food chicken place two days; he really did not like that job.

One day, my mom called home around noon and he answered the phone. He had spent the morning watching soap operas and had not begun his job search for the day. (This was back when you couldn't just search for jobs on the Internet.) I'm not sure of the exact words that my mom used when she spoke with him, but I know that he got up and started moving after he hung up the phone with her.

You are your greatest asset. But, sometimes you must move your ASSets. Just like my brother got up and found a job (that day by the way,) you should move your assets in such a way that you find income or additional income to balance your budget, get out of debt, save money for college or retirement, start a business, or whatever other goal that you have set for yourself.

So yes, leave your daddy a note. But, the bible is very clear that faith without works is dead. So, after you leave your daddy a note, start taking the necessary steps so that you can travel this journey effectively. Read the words that are printed in the book and do the work that is required for you to successfully travel down this journey to financial freedom.

There may be roadblocks, there may be detours, and you may get distracted. When you do, consider this book to be your SIRI. This book can serve as your GPS, so that when you start traveling on your journey to financial freedom and you take a detour, rerouting can take place. Just pick back up where you are, and get back on your journey.

Chapter 2

Stewardship Street   2ND

Now that you understand the importance of having a Millionaire's Mindset and, by relationship with God, you already have the Millionaire in you; it is time to start the journey. This first street on your journey to financial freedom is Stewardship Street. You might consider this the main street from which every other road on the journey feeds from. It is here on Stewardship Street that you will learn what your role is as a steward of God's resources.

What is a steward, you ask? A steward is a manager. You are a steward of the resources that God has blessed you with. These resources could be tangible things such as money, family, your home, and other material possessions, or intangible things such as your talents, gifts, and your knowledge.

Whether tangible or intangible, God expects us to be good stewards of ALL the resources He has given us. I Corinthians 4:2 states, "Moreover, it is required in stewards that a man be found faithful."

Becoming a better steward of your finances usually requires that you become a better steward over other things. For example, if you are in sales or own businesses where you earn money by the amount of time that you spend being productive in your work, you must be a better steward of your time to increase your income.

Students, if you want to pursue a rewarding career in the future, or start your own business, you must be a good steward of the time and attention that you spend learning; so that you will have the knowledge to pursue your dreams.

To better recognize your role as a steward, take a moment to complete the *Quit Claim Deed*. In this deed, you take the time to write out the things you are currently a steward over. I've included a sample with just a few things to get your mind thinking. However, remember that this is your proclamation and acknowledgement to God that you are the manager; and not the owner of the things you list. Please take a few minutes to complete your *Quit Claim Deed.*

SAMPLE QUIT CLAIM DEED

I, **Angela Dees**, as Grantor, remise, remit and forever quit claim to God, the following:

My tangible assets: home, car, clothes, jewelry, money
My relationships: husband, child, family, friends
My intangible assets: thoughts, fears, education, abilities, health, knowledge, victories

I recognize that I am merely a steward of these things and that God is the true owner.
Signed this, **7th**, day of **July, 2017**.

Angela Dees_____   *Angela Dees*_____
Your Name Printed Here   Your Signature Here

Kevin Dees_____   *Kevin Dees*_____
Witness Name Printed Here   Witness Signature Here

YOUR QUIT CLAIM DEED

I, _____, as Grantor, remise, remit and forever quit claim to God, the following:

My tangible assets: _____, _____, _____, _____
My relationships: _____, _____, _____, _____
My intangible assets: _____, _____, _____, _____

I recognize that I am merely a steward of these things and that God is the true owner.
Signed this, _____, day of _____, 20_____.

_____   _____
Your Name Printed Here   Your Signature Here

_____   _____
Witness Name Printed Here   Witness Signature Here

Now that you've listed all the things that you are a manager of, it is important to keep this thought in your mind. While you continue your journey to financial freedom, take the time daily to learn and meditate on the following verse. This verse will help you keep this journey in perspective and empower you when you hit any road blocks or detours.

"Everything in the heavens and earth is yours, O Lord, and this is your kingdom. We adore you as being in control of everything. Riches and honor come from you alone, and you are the Ruler of all mankind: your hand controls power and might, and it is at your discretion that men are made great and given strength."

(I Chronicles 29:11-12 LB)

Giving Gateway

Now that you understand stewardship and know that you are simply managers of the resources that God has given you, it's time to go through Giving Gateway.

Wait! What? Give?

Yes, you read it correctly. Give.

You've read your Bible; you know, or at least have heard, what it says in Acts 20:35: "Remember the words of the Lord Jesus, that He Himself said, It is more blessed to give than receive." You might say, "But why is it more blessed? I want to be the one being blessed." Well, if you've ever given of yourself, your time, energy, or service in an earnest and sincere way to an individual, or perhaps an organization that was in need of help, you know that you usually get more out of the experience than the receiver does. I believe giving is the gateway in your journey to financial freedom because it helps put things in perspective. When you give, you have the privilege of getting yourself out of the way, for a moment, to put someone else's needs before yours. It helps you to be less selfish and become more selfless.

I am part of a giving family. Every Christmas, my brothers, Kelvin and Rodney Hampton, spearhead *A Better Bail Bond,* and *Hamp's Camp Annual Christmas Bike Drive* where we give away bikes to underprivileged youth in the Houston area. We raise money throughout the year so that we can give bikes to the youth in need. When we give those bikes, so many lives are touched: youth from homeless shelters; youth whose parents are in jail; youth whose moms have been victims of domestic violence; or simply youth whose parents were just a little short on money and couldn't afford to grant them their Christmas wish of having a new bike. You cannot box up the feeling of gratitude of the kids and parents who receive these bikes. You also cannot box up the joy, peace, and feelings of worthiness that I feel in being a part of such a wonderful event.

Why does that matter as you go along this journey to becoming a millionaire? In my opinion, giving helps you build that *Millionaire Mindset* we talked about earlier. It also helps you to keep things in perspective. This journey is about you, but not just about you. I believe that you are on this journey to financial freedom so that you can be freed up to be a blessing to others.

Open and Closed Fist Illustration

After all, you've heard the story about the open and closed fist. Make a tight fist with your hand right now. Squeeze it as hard as you can. Look at it. If this fist represented your financial attitude towards giving, how would you describe it? Is it tight? Is it available? Are you protecting what's there? When you have a closed fist—when you're closed to giving—it is true that no money can leave your hand. But have you considered the opposite? If someone was trying to place a $100 bill into your closed fist, could they? Now, open that closed fist. Go ahead, open it. Now, I have the same question for you. Even though your hand is open and available to give, you are also now in a posture to receive.

Tithing

Biblically, you are taught to give a tithe (10 percent of your increase). You may say that God doesn't need your money. You're right. He doesn't. He needs to know that you trust Him to give you all that you need. When you think back to our last stop, Stewardship Street, you can really understand what a great deal it is. God owns everything— even your money. He gives it to you and simply asks that you give Him back 10 cents of every dollar so that He knows you trust Him to take care of your needs.

In Malachi 3:10-11, it states, "Bring all the tithes into the storehouse, That there may be food in My house, And try Me now in this, Says the Lord of host, If I will not open for you the windows of heaven and pour out for you such blessing that there will not be room enough to receive it. And I will rebuke the devourer for your sakes, So that he will not destroy the fruit of your ground. Nor shall the vine fail to bear fruit for you in the field, says the Lord of hosts."

You may have been taught to tithe but don't. If that is the case, have you ever wondered why you can never seem to keep money? It is clear, in Malachi—the devourer is taking your money and destroying your productivity. Tithing will not end your financial blues overnight, but it is an important step to acknowledge your understanding of who is truly in control.

Maybe you haven't been taught about tithing. Well, now you have.

What if you're not a Christian and you don't believe in God or giving?

My prayer is that you will come into a relationship with God and grow in your understanding of giving. However, I still feel the benefits of giving opens the gateway on your journey to financial freedom. I still feel that it helps keep your mind in the right perspective of knowing that although this is your journey, it is not just about you.

Giving is also not just about money; you can give your time, service, and gifts. It is very empowering to give because, when you give, you make yourself available to receive.

Work Walkway

Work Walkway

This next stop on the journey to financial freedom is often the most misunderstood and abused area of financial stewardship. You may feel that you work for your employer. The reality is, however, that you work for God. Just look at Colossians 3:23, 24 where it reads, "Whatever you do, do your work heartily, as for the Lord rather than for men; knowing that from the Lord you will receive the reward of the inheritance. It is the Lord Christ whom you serve."

Yes, even at work you must be a good steward of the talents that God has given you. Your employer's name may be the name on your paycheck, but you represent God while you're at work. Are you making God look bad? Do you work hard only when your employer or supervisor is watching? Or do you work heartily no matter what? Be honest. Do you treat your job like you own the company? Or are you haphazard in completing your work, doing just enough to get by? If you own a business or supervise others, do you treat them with respect? Or do you treat your employees like dirt? Be honest.

Take this challenge for the next week at work and see if it doesn't change your perspective. Each day, ask yourself, "How would God want me to conduct myself at work?" Ask yourself that question at work each day. When you take on this perspective in your work, you can't help but be a better steward in your work. Then, you will see some amazing results.

If you are a young adult and don't have a paying job, apply this same principle to your role as a student. Being a good student is your job right now. Do you just do good work in class when you are forced to? Do you have a schedule for getting your assignments completed? Are you putting your best effort forward, or are you spending most of your day on social media and allowing your focus to be diverted by other things? No judgment. I just want you to recognize that your journey to financial freedom doesn't start after you finish school; it starts with the efforts you put into getting your education right now.

Finally, you must remember to avoid the other extreme as well—becoming a workaholic. Simply put, if God needed a day to rest after creating the world, then you need a day to rest too. Take it. Enjoy it.

Know your assignment

Make a list of some things that excited you when you were younger. Did you enjoy cooking with your mom? Did you like math in school? Or, was history your favorite subject? My friend and prayer partner, Kim Porter, wrote a book called *The Assignment*. One thing that she consistently talks about is enjoying your work. She says, "I don't think God meant for us to spend 40 or more hours each week doing something that we hate." Do you look forward to your work? If not, maybe it's time for you to figure out your Assignment so that your journey on Work Walkway can be one filled with joy and financial peace.

Beware of laziness

Not truly knowing your real assignment, however, doesn't give you an excuse to be lazy simply because you are not currently doing the work that you are called to do. Proverbs 10:4 states, "He becometh poor that dealeth with a slack hand; but the hand of the diligent maketh rich." You often want to whine about what you don't have, cry about how life is unfair to you, or compare yourselves to other people, and your possessions to theirs. In some cases, however, your lack is not because life has dealt you a bad hand, or because God has singled you out for discipline. Often, your *lack* is due to your *slack.* You say you want nice cars, nice things, increase, more money, more freedom; but you don't put in the necessary work to have it. You want phenomenal income to come from ordinary efforts. You want an extraordinary life-style but you work in a mediocre way. Verse 5 of Proverbs 10 goes on to say, "He that gathereth in summer is a wise son: but he that sleepeth in harvest is a son that causeth shame." Simply put, don't sleep when you should be working. Get up and work! Yes, you could look at this figuratively and say that summer is the harvest time and, during the harvest, work hard. Or, you may think that you only need to work when it matters or when it *counts.*

Imagine if Michael Jordan felt that way. What type of player do you think he would have been if he had only worked on his basketball game during the playoffs? Would he have even made it to the play offs? No, Michael Jordan, or any other great athlete, knows the importance of working, even when it seems that no one is watching. How about Bill Gates? Do you feel he built the Microsoft empire by only working some of the time or half-heartedly? Oprah Winfrey? Do you think she sleeps until noon and then gets up, hoping to pull off her best show ever?

Laziness is such a subtle trait. I know, because I had to recognize it and deal with it in my own work ethic. I would think, "Oh, I can get to that tomorrow. Maybe I'll just go to lunch with my sister; then, I'll come back and finish. Oh, a quick nap before I wrap up my day won't matter." It does. On the other hand, when I'm diligent in my work, watch out. I'll do more before 10:00 a.m. than most people do all day. I will start with a plan of what I want to accomplish, begin my day with devotion so that I can be prayerful about how God wants to lead me that day, and approach the day with a great attitude, knowing that I will be productive in ways that I couldn't have dreamed of.

Work Walkway can be the most rewarding, or the most frustrating, part on your journey to discovering the millionaire within. However, if you do your work as if God were your supervisor, and if you work with diligence and put your heart into it, then you will reap a great harvest.

My Work Walkway Story

Work walkway was the most difficult road to travel on my journey to bring out the millionaire in me. It was difficult because I started my career doing exactly what I love to do. I worked in the financial services industry, helping people save for college, retirement, and whatever other long-term goals they told me they had. I loved the fact that because people sat with me, their kids would be able to go to college, they would be able to retire early or at the least comfortably, and if in the unfortunate event they died prematurely, most of the goals they set for their family would still be achievable through the life insurance funds from the policies we had put in place.

In addition to the fulfillment that I received from helping families and businesses, I also enjoyed a rather flexible schedule. I worked primarily by appointments. Since I avoided traffic like the plague, that generally meant my first appointment was around 9:30 or 10 and my last appointment was about 2:00 or 3:00 in the afternoon. I spent the early morning and late afternoons doing service, prospecting, and preparation work. How great was that? I saw my son off to school every day, and was usually home when he got back in the afternoon.

So, what was so difficult for me about work walkway? I enjoyed what I was doing, and I had a great schedule that afforded me the opportunity to be there for my son and family. What was the problem? One word—Commissions!

I worked primarily on commission pay. This meant that during the times when I was more work-focused and kept a consistent schedule, my paycheck over the next month or two reflected that—usually in a very good way. However, the converse was also true. During those times when I took time off to travel, or enjoy the holidays, or when I just did not have as many appointments (during the summer for instance), the few months following those times were frugal.

For nearly 11 years, I struggled with the constant battle of trying to even out my cash flow. Sure, my income increased over the years. I even built up a modest base of income through renewals after being with my last employer for a few years; however, the fluctuations in income took their toll. In one month, for example, I might earn between $3,000 and $6,000 whereas the next month I might earn between $300 and $600. I had read and even supported the philosophy that is taught to commission workers about taking the income from the good months and spreading it out over the times when business is seasonal or slower. However, with the debt load that we had at the time, I simply could not afford to have slow months. It seemed that when I did have a couple of good months, I was always playing catch-up for the months that were slow.

I was stubborn. I was determined. I was convinced that since I enjoyed what I did so much, that it would just be a matter of time before I figured out how to make it work. I wasn't just going to make it work. I was going to make it work my way. I would keep my "Mommy" hours. I would still have my travel. I would still take off some time during the summer and during the holidays. Not!!!

I was fed up. The very career I loved so much started feeling more like work. It was hard to convince my clients about what they should do with their money when I struggled with my inconsistent income. So, I did something I thought I would never do. I got a regular job!

It was great! Every week I got a check. Every week I cashed a check. Every week, I could now budget what would get paid, what I would save for taxes, what fun money I would have. It was a liberating experience. Now, I'm sure that for many this sounds insane. What is so great about a regular paycheck? Trust me, you can only truly relate if you haven't had one.

I mean, from a big picture perspective, I made the same money if not less than I did in my sales position in financial services. However, from a budgeting perspective, I feel like my salary was doubled because I could plan how my funds would come in and go out of the household.

More importantly, with income from a regular job, I still had the option of supplementing that income with additional work. So, now I had a regular income, plus supplemental income for the fun stuff. Life was good!

Work walkway, however, is not just about a regular job and consistent income to balance a budget. Work walkway is about dedicating the time that you work, and the type of work you do, to God. After all, we are encouraged to "do your work heartily as for the Lord rather than men, because it is the Lord Jesus that we serve."

I would not change my work experience for anything. I have always known that my career in financial services was really an avenue and training ground for me to do something great for God. I have always treated my work as a ministry. So many people struggle with money because they have the wrong perspective. They think the money belongs to them. So many couples end up in divorce because they don't unite around the mentality of shared funds and because they are not in agreement regarding who the money truly belongs to.

I know that even during my time as a teacher, God used me to influence youth to attain a better life, both spiritually and financially. I know this because this is how he wired me. He made me love numbers from the time I was a child. He made me a "know it all" who likes telling people what to do and watching them be successful. So, whether it is in the conference room or the classroom, I know that I am walking in God's purpose through my work.

Honesty Highway

Honesty Highway

So, why is a place like Honesty Highway included in a book about bringing out the millionaire in you?

<u>Be honest with yourself</u>

Thank you for asking. It is included because you will really have to be honest with yourself if you are going to be successful on this journey. You have to honestly determine if you are willing to do the work. Do you have the courage to travel down Budget Boardwalk and make the necessary changes to your current spending pattern? Do you have the courage to stroll down Insurance Lane and do the work of reviewing and making the right changes to existing plans? So, by being honest with yourself, although at first it may be a little challenging, will help this journey to take place on the HIGHway.

<u>Be honest with others</u>

In addition to being honest with yourself, you have to be honest with the other people in your life about what you are doing. This may require that you let your friends know that you are choosing not to meet them for lunch twice a week because you have decided to save money and bring leftovers. This may require you to tell your children that they have to work and do chores to earn their allowance for some of the extras. Yes, this is your journey, but it will affect other people in your life.

Be honest with God

If this is hard for you, it's okay. Let God know where you are and that you need strength and courage. He is there for you. He is your light and your salvation—whom shall you fear? The LORD is the stronghold of your life—of whom shall you be afraid? Psalm 27:1-2 (NIV paraphrased)

Counsel Court

Counsel Court

Proverbs 12:15 states, "The way of a fool is right in his own eyes, but a wise man is he who listens to counsel."

You're not alone. I'm putting Counsel Court at this place because I know that your success depends on having an accountability partner, good coaching, and the right resources. This is why I have included all of that information on my website, bringoutthemillionaire.com. So, as you prepare for Budget Boardwalk, Debt Free Drive, and the remaining stops on this journey, there is no need to feel overwhelmed. This book will give you an overview and steps to take, but if you need additional assistance, wherever you are on your journey, go to bringoutthe millionaire.com, click on where you are in your journey, and you will have access to interactive worksheets to help you get the work done in a quick and efficient manner. For each area, there is also a wealth of resources and quick links so that you can BRING OUT THE MILLIONAIRE.

Seeking counsel/advice from someone does not mean you are WEAK or WEIRD. The first source of counsel should be THE BIBLE (Basic Instructions Before Leaving Earth), then your SPOUSE (if you are married), PARENTS (if you are single), then trusted advisors.

DON'T BE A FOOL.

Now, let's move on to Budget Boardwalk.

Chapter 3

Budget Boardwalk

3RD

Oh, No!!! The evil word—BUDGET. Don't even sweat this. Establishing and maintaining a budget is very simple and can be summarized in one simple phrase:

Spend less than you earn and save the rest.

It really is that simple. The reason that simple things get complicated is because you don't do them. You spend what you earn, what you are about to earn, and what you think you will earn. You save IF there is something left. Then you go back and spend that too. You know it is the truth. If you don't do this, congratulations, go to the next chapter—you're good. But if you've done this to some extent, or you want to review your present budget, finish this chapter.

There are hundreds, possibly thousands, of books on personal finances. In Kelvin Boston's *Smart Money Moves,* however, he does a good job of explaining how to develop a budget. He refers to a concept introduced by Mark and Jo Ann Skousen, authors of *High Finance on a Low Budget,* where they talk about the *"No Budget, Budget."* The instructions are simply to note every dollar spent for 21 days and analyze the expenditures. Mark and JoAnn contend that if you can figure out where you are overspending, then you can simply cut down on those expenses, and the rest will fall in place. This works.

In addition, you should look at the areas where you are overspending and pray over the root issue, because there usually is one. For example, when I did this exercise years ago, I noticed that I was spending a lot on food. When I prayed about it, I realized I was using food to escape problems or issues I may have had by treating myself to a nice dinner (an expensive one usually). Maybe it is not food for you. Maybe you indulge in *retail therapy* as a means of escape or just to make yourself feel better. Possibly you spend more, and drink more alcohol, than you ordinarily do when you are not stressed. Or maybe you spend more money on your children than you realize and, when you really think about it, you might be overcompensating for your feeling of lack from your childhood. I'm not a psychologist, but I do know that taking the time to reflect over why you are spending what you do can be life changing and may result in you taking bold, positive steps in balancing your budget.

Be realistic

One reason that budgeting doesn't work for you is because it is unrealistic. You want to be as realistic as possible when you are putting together your budget. Ladies, if you know you are going to go shopping at least once a month, don't just budget $10 for shopping. Men, if you know you're going to play golf or hang out with your friends, plan for it. Students, if you know that you are going to that big party, be realistic; put it in your budget.

Be prayerful

Start praying about your spending decisions. In Matthew 6:33 it states, "Seek first the kingdom of God and His righteousness, and all these things shall be added to you." God is interested in how you spend the resources He has provided for you, so involve God in your spending decisions.

Make it a family affair

If you are married, set a date to review this information with your spouse. This takes the burden off of just one person and helps to create a team approach when setting goals and executing the plan. If you have children, get them involved too. Children get their first money class by watching what you do as parents. Simply helping them to understand the cost of the activities that they are involved in can help shape their perspective about money.

Set some clear goals

In addition to looking at your current budget, it is also important to set some financial goals that may impact your current budget. These goals should be clear goals with specific amounts and time frames. For example, maybe you have a goal to take a vacation next year. You've traveled before and you know that the vacation you're interested in will cost about $3,000. If you plan to take the trip in a year, then a clear goal may look like this:

GOAL	Total $ Amount	TIME	Monthly $ Amount
Vacation	$3,000	12 months	$250/month

Now, take the time to establish at least 3 financial goals that you want to accomplish in the next year.

GOAL	Total $ Amount	Monthly $ Amount
1._____	$_____	$_____
2._____	$_____	$_____
3._____	$_____	$_____

I want you to have this list because, as you create your budget, you want to incorporate these goals into it.

Even as you make these goals, be sure to be realistic in your planning; unrealistic goals will affect your budget. If your budget is too strict, unrealistic, or too confining, it will inevitably fail.

Now that you have some clear goals set, it is time to start the work of developing your budget.

What you earn

At this point, on Budget Boardwalk, you need to make a list of what you earn. The simplest way to do this is to write out what your gross pay is, if you are a W-2 employee. If you have the last paystub of your previous year available, this will give you the annualized amount. If you are a 1099 contract worker and you have a base income, then write that gross monthly amount as well.

Variable/Sporadic Income

In addition to your base salary, you may earn bonuses or commissions. For bonuses that you earn once a year, estimate the amount and divide it by 12. If you work on commission, look at your annual commissions for the previous year and divide by 12 to get a monthly estimated amount to include in your budget. You might also earn extra income from other sources. Again, since this amount varies, review what you earned over the last 12 months and divide that amount by 12 as well.

Use the table below to record what you earn on a monthly and annual basis.

WHAT YOU EARN

	ANNUALLY	MONTHLY
Salary	$_____	$_____
1099 Income	$_____	$_____
Bonuses	$_____	$_____
Commissions	$_____	$_____
Other	$_____	$_____
TOTAL INCOME	$_____	$_____

To put this directly into a template, simply go to bringout themillionaire.com and click on Budget Boardwalk. There you can either complete the information in the link provided or you can print the full-page, print ready template to complete by hand.

Next, on Budget Boardwalk, you will review what you spend.

What you spend

First, you want to go back to your paystub, if you are a W-2 employee, and list the amounts that are taken out of your gross income. This includes social security, federal, Medicare, and possibly state taxes. Fill in the total taxes in that category of the budget template. You may also have deductions for your retirement savings, insurance, credit union, or other savings plans. Likewise, put those amounts in the appropriate categories of your budget template.

Use one of the following strategies to complete the remainder of the categories on this part of the budget template.

1. Go through each category and estimate the amount you spend based on what you know the bills to be.

2. If you use a debit or credit cards regularly, you can use those statements or download your transactions directly from your bank to get the specifics for what you spend in each category of your budget.

3. If you don't use your debit or credit cards regularly, then you can still use your bank statements, but you may also have to review cancelled checks or your actual billing statements to get an accurate picture of what you are spending monthly.

No matter which of these three methods you use to complete your initial budget, I highly recommend using the 21-day journaling of income and expenses that I mentioned earlier. This process will help you to raise your awareness of where you are spending or possibly overspending. However, I do not want you to delay completing your budget for 21 days. So, for now, choose one of the three methods above so that you can complete the remainder of your budget. After you complete journaling your income and expenses for at least 21 days, you can go back and see if the budget you created currently is a good reflection of what you are earning and spending. You will also have a better idea of how you are spending your cash and can adjust the budget you are creating now at that time.

The list below is a summarized version of what you spend. You can simply use pencil and paper to calculate the totals for each category to place here. If you would like to use the more detailed template from the beginning, use the full page, print ready template provided on the website, bringoutthemillionaire.com.

Use the information you have gathered about each of your expense categories to complete the WHAT YOU SPEND table below.

WHAT YOU SPEND

	ANNUALLY	MONTHLY
TITHE/GIVING	$_____	$_____
SAVINGS	$_____	$_____
INVESTMENTS	$_____	$_____
INSURANCE	$_____	$_____
HOME	$_____	$_____
FOOD	$_____	$_____
CAR	$_____	$_____
DEBTS	$_____	$_____
LEISURE/TRAVEL	$_____	$_____
CLOTHING	$_____	$_____
MEDICAL	$_____	$_____
EDUCATION	$_____	$_____
MISCELLANEOUS	$_____	$_____
TOTAL EXPENSES	$_____	$_____

You know WHAT YOU EARN and WHAT YOU SPEND, so now you just need to put it all together.

Putting it all together

WHAT YOU EARN

	ANNUALLY	MONTHLY
Salary/Pension	$_____	$_____
1099 Income	$_____	$_____
Bonuses	$_____	$_____
Commissions	$_____	$_____
Other	$_____	$_____
TOTAL INCOME	$_____	$_____

WHAT YOU SPEND

	ANNUALLY	MONTHLY
TAXES	$_____	$_____
TITHE/GIVING	$_____	$_____
SAVINGS	$_____	$_____
INVESTMENTS	$_____	$_____
INSURANCE	$_____	$_____
HOME	$_____	$_____
FOOD	$_____	$_____
CAR	$_____	$_____
DEBTS	$_____	$_____
LEISURE/TRAVEL	$_____	$_____
CLOTHING	$_____	$_____
MEDICAL	$_____	$_____
EDUCATION	$_____	$_____
MISCELLANEOUS	$_____	$_____
TOTAL EXPENSES	$_____	$_____
SURPLUS (DEFICIT)	$_____	$_____

THE REST

Surplus

When you created your budget, if your income exceeded your expenses, you have a surplus. Congratulations! You may still need to make some adjustments to your budget so that you can have an even greater surplus for saving or investing. Or, maybe you noticed that you are still overspending in a certain category, and you want to be more aggressive in getting rid of debt, increase giving, or maybe expanding your travel plans.

Deficit

If you had more month than money when you created your budget, then you have two choices. You either need to reduce your expenses or you must increase income. Before I go through the list of budgeting tips that you can take to reduce your expenses, I want you to first consider how you can earn additional income. Then, simply choose one thing and write out the first three steps that you need to do to begin earning income. Some examples might be tutoring, becoming a part-time driver, lawn care, babysitting, or additional contract work. The possibilities are endless. So, don't overthink it. You are simply considering an extra income opportunity that you can do for a short while until you get your budget balanced. Once you have nailed down just one thing, write it here:

Income Possibility: I will earn additional income by _____
_____.

Now that you have pinned down what you want to do, I want you to write down, in three steps, what you need to do to start making that happen. Please be specific.

For example, if you plan to earn extra money selling cakes, your action steps may be:

1. Buy ingredients (eggs, milk, flour, pans, etc.)
2. Develop menu (2 or 3 cakes for what price)
3. Advertise (Facebook, email blast, fliers)

Action steps:
1. _____
2. _____
3. _____

I like to start with earning extra income because there is usually something you can do to earn extra income right away. If you decide to earn this additional income, I want you to open a separate account; place only the money earned from that extra work in that account. Then, at the end of 30 days, you can use that money to pay down credit card balances or other items that may be causing your budget to be out of balance. By the way, if you listed some opportunities that you are really passionate about and you think you might want to convert them into a home-based business down the line, pick up *Giving Birth to Your Home-Based Business* by Debbie Porter, my sister. (Shameless plug, I know. www.bookdebbieporter.com)

Reducing expenses

The best way to tackle reducing expenses is to take one category at a time. This list is designed to prompt you to think about areas in each category that you may need to review or revamp altogether. This list is designed as a reference. You may not need to implement every suggestion for your personal budget, but read through each category anyway—the suggestions may help you to come up with some creative solutions of your own.

Home

- Review your current mortgage to determine if your interest rate is too high. Refinancing may be an option for you.
- Review any maintenance contracts to determine if you need to make changes.
- Maybe have the cleaning lady come less often instead of cancelling altogether.
- It may be time to start cutting your own grass.
- Have you compared the rates of your utility companies lately?

Home Mortgage Payment Tip

If you have a higher mortgage payment, you may consider breaking up the payment in two, and having that amount automatically deducted from your bank account into a separate bank account when you get paid; then, you can have the mortgage company deduct the total directly from that separate account. This will help to even out your cash-flow by allowing you to save smaller amounts from each check.

Auto

- Did you buy too much car? If so, would selling it and buying a less expensive car be an option?
- Review auto insurance coverages—even if you have a decent rate now.
- Check for less expensive fuel options.
- Consider paying your car note weekly instead of monthly to pay it off quicker.
- If you're considering purchasing a car, calculate what the estimated payment will be, and pay it to a savings account for three months to assure yourself that you can afford the note. This will help you to know if this is a purchase your budget can handle, and it will help you develop a reserve for future car maintenance.

Food

- Cooking can still save you money. Maybe eat out just twice a week instead of three to four times.
- Can couponing work for you? Have you tried it recently?
- Make a list before going to the grocery store.
- Do you have to have that Starbucks every day? Maybe a coffee maker at home is a better option. Or, if you already have one, maybe ordering bulk coffee saves you significantly.

Debts

- Pay off your debts (more on that on Debt Free Drive).
- Call your credit card companies and ask for a lower rate, especially if you've been a good paying customer and you've had the credit card for a long time.
- Use cash.

Insurance

- Purchase insurance for your most important assets (more on that on Insurance Lane).
- Compare quotes with at least 3 companies.
- Stop smoking. This will help lower your rates for different types of insurance.

Leisure/travel

- Plan for leisure and travel. You work all year; you need this time to reboot.
- A good travel agent can save you money. Ask around when planning your trips.
- If you're booking plane tickets or hotels, use the air travel sites to compare rates.
- Groupon can be your friend for planning fun activities at a discount.

Medical

- Compare prescription prices between pharmacies.
- Ask your physician for samples if you have prescriptions that are too expensive (or if you're a senior and fall in the gap a few times a year).
- Review your health insurance coverage annually to make sure it will have the coverage and the doctors you want.

Education

- Start saving early for college.
- Apply for scholarships (whether it is for you or your children).
- Compare college costs.
- Compare private school vs public school for your area.

Miscellaneous

- Track your cash spending to identify where it is going.
- Use the 21-day journal to get a handle on those miscellaneous purchases.

Obviously, you will not need or desire to use all the suggestions listed in the previous categories but, hopefully, the list has triggered a few ideas for you to act on right away. I would also like for you to share some of your best budgeting tips with me. Email me at info@bringoutthemillionaire.com and share your best budgeting tip.

Now, let's continue your journey and address an area that, when corrected, can be one of the best ways to get your budget balanced— Debt Free Drive.

Chapter 4

Debt Free Drive 4TH

Don't Even Buy That

Zero down, zero payments, zero interest for one year—Don't Even Buy That! Need new furniture? No money, no payments for 6 months—Don't Even Buy That! Taking a vacation? Just charge it; pay it off in a year—Don't Even Buy That! Need some clothes? Oh, yes, NEED some clothes. Have to INVEST in your image so that you can be more successful. Yes, well, it's okay to charge that, right? Don't Even Buy That!

It is said that we are about to experience the greatest transfer of wealth to ever take place—the Baby Boomers' parents are changing their address to heaven and leaving these huge inheritances. Many speculate that it will be an infusion of capital in the economy, and will sort of help this world to get back on track. But, upon closer examination, it's clear that most of this legacy money will not be used to start new businesses or invest in homes. Most of this money will be used to pay the masters off.

You know the masters: VISA, *Master*card, American Express, Student Loans, and 2nd Mortgage. You know. The things that keep us from serving the one true Master, faithfully. You know the Masters: the ones that compete for your attention. You know, God is jealous of them because you put your faith in them. You allow yourself to be servants to them, and God knows that you can't serve two masters. So, He waits for you to surrender.

God is waiting for you to fess up to your mistakes. Hold your hands up and give it to Him. Now, don't go there. He doesn't want you to just sit and wait for Him to do everything. He wants you to face your fears. Write your debts down. Seek HIS guidance about the right plan of action and MOVE YOUR FEET, not just your LIPS.

You can't give up your cable TV? **D**on't **E**ven **B**uy **T**hat! You can't live without a cell phone? **D**on't **E**ven **B**uy **T**hat! You are so far in debt, there is no way you can get out of it. **D**on't **E**ven **B**uy **T**hat!

Start where you are right now. God is still God. What a mountain is to you, is not even a molehill to Him. Seek. Listen. Obey. Surrender. Act!!!

The Masters

Debt-Free Drive is such a crucial part on your journey to financial freedom because it will free you from the bondage that is keeping you from realizing your true millionaire potential!

Proverbs 22:7 says, "The rich rule over the poor, and the borrower is servant to the lender." Let's look at that more closely with the help of Webster's New World Thesaurus, 1974.

Rich— (possession of wealth) wealthy, moneyed, well-off, well provided for, worth a million, (fertile) fruit bearing, abundant, yielding
Rule v.—control, regulate (manage), lead, oversee, instruct, show, disburse, distribute, handle, watch, guide, supervise, conduct, engage in
Over—aloft, overhead, up, beyond, higher than, further than
Poor— (lacking worldly goods) indigent, penniless, moneyless, needy, poverty-stricken, underprivileged, ill-provided, in want, hard-up, down and out
And—in addition to, also, plus, moreover
Borrow—v. sponge, go into debt, accept the loan of, gets temporary use of, use, rent, hire, obtain;   borrower—person who does these things
Servant—n. dependent, slave, attendant
Serve—v. labor, obey the call, pay one's debt
Lend—v. advance, provide with, let out, furnish, permit to borrow, extend credit, accommodate, lend on; security lender—n. person who does this

So, the fruit-bearing, well-provided for, moneyed, millionaire, regulates and controls what the penniless, hard-up, ill-provided for person does; in addition, the person who sponges from, accepts the loan of, or goes into debt, becomes the **slave**, dependent, and attendant of the person providing, furnishing, and accommodating the funds.

Slave, what is your master's name?—VISA, Mastercard, American Express, JC Penny's, Macy's, Goodyear, Sears, your mother, father, sister.

I know, this is even harsh for me to read. But, I want you to develop a distaste for debt, so I am intentionally emphasizing that you become a slave to the lenders that you send payments to. I've done it too. Zero payments; zero down; it can work. It has worked for me sometimes because, in all honesty, if you are able to pull off a zero down, zero payments deal during the promotional period, you win. The bigger problem is the retail debt—the convenience of charging and paying later. Once again, if you pay your credit card bill off monthly, you still win. But the danger comes when something else creeps in and, all of sudden, you are unable to pay it off like you expected to. When you carry debt with the interest rates that are charged by most banks and credit card companies, and you don't pay it off, they win. More often than not, they win. They lure you into paying only the minimum balance so that they can make all the interest from your credit. You tell yourself you are going to pay it off, but something else gets your attention—a vacation you must take or an opportunity you must take advantage of. So, even if you pay off your original balance, there is more debt accumulated. Now, if you have significant assets and can choose at any time to pay off your debt, these balances are not as dangerous. But, if you are barely letting your month equal your money, you need to break free of *the masters* as soon as possible.

I want to be clear; being in debt is not sin. It may, however, stifle you from being able to do all that God wants you to do. Now, if you are in debt, you can do one of two things: 1) You can have a pity party and come down on yourself for all the reasons why you're in debt; or 2) you can develop a plan of action and attack!

Breaking free

It's time to break free of the debt. Before you can break free, however, you must commit to not accumulate any new consumer debt. So, let's start by taking off the chains. Any good pair of scissors will do. Take your credit cards and cut them up. Until you have taken off the chains of debt, you need to cut up your credit cards and commit to paying cash for all upcoming and unplanned expenses.

This means that you will need to create a reserve fund rather quickly. Earlier, on Budget Boardwalk, I asked you to come up with several ways that you can earn extra money. Now, I want you to go back to those possibilities and choose one. Then, if you haven't already, I want you to open an online bank account to deposit this extra money into. This will be the start of your emergency fund. Initially, I want you to make a goal of saving at least $1,000 in your reserve fund. Having this reserve will be a great start to keeping you from needing your credit cards. Long term, you should establish a goal of accumulating at least 3 to 6 months of income for a more adequate reserve.

Once you have created a stream of income to build an emergency fund, gather a list of your debts. If you've done the work on Budget Boardwalk, you probably already have most of your debt information. Use the Sample Debt List below as a guide to complete Your Debt List on the following page. For each debt, please list who the debtor is (who you make the check payable to), interest rate charged, minimum payment, and the balance.

SAMPLE DEBT LIST			
Creditor	Amount Owed	Monthly Payment	Interest Rate%
Visa	$450	$150	18%
Mastercard	$470	$30	15%
AMEX	$300	$20	10%

Angela Dees

YOUR DEBT LIST			
Creditor	Amount Owed	Monthly Payment	Interest Rate
	$	$	%
	$	$	%
	$	$	%
	$	$	%
	$	$	%
	$	$	%

Create your Debt elimination plan now

Now that you have made a list of your debts, it's time to create your debt elimination plan. You want to pay off the debt with the lowest balance/highest interest rate first; then you can redirect the money that you were paying to that debt and add it to the next debt. When you pay off the lowest balance first, this will give you a sense of accomplishment and, since you were already paying that bill, you can easily apply that payment to the next debt on the list.

I have included a sample of how this would work in the following debt elimination plan.

SAMPLE DEBT ELIMINATION PLAN

Date		Amount	Creditor		Balance
1/1		$150	Visa		$300
1/1		$30	Mastercard		$470
1/1		$20	AMEX		$300
	Total	$200		Total	$1070
2/1		$150	Visa		$150
2/1		$30	Mastercard		$440
2/1		$20	AMEX		$280
	Total	$200		Total	$870
3/1		$150	Visa		$0
3/1		$30	Mastercard		$410
3/1		$20	AMEX		$260
	Total	$200		Total	$670
4/1		$180	Mastercard		$230
4/1		$20	AMEX		$240
	Total	$200		Total	$470
5/1		$180	Mastercard		$50
5/1		$20	AMEX		$220
	Total	$200		Total	$270
6/1		$50	Mastercard		$0
6/1		$150	AMEX		$70
	Total	$200		Total	$70
7/1		$70	AMEX		$0
7/1		$130	Giving Gateway		$130
	Total	$200		Total	$130

In the example, you can notice that in month 3, the Visa bill was paid in full; so, in month 4, that $150 was added to the Mastercard payment and, instead of paying just $30, $180 was paid. This pattern was repeated in month 6, but this time the balance on the Mastercard was only $50. So now, only $50 of the $180 was used to pay Mastercard, and the additional $130 was added to the AMEX payment.

If you have small balances on different cards, you will be surprised to see how easily you can quickly pay off your credit cards, especially if you have committed to not increasing your consumer debt. I have provided a blank template here for you to make copies of and use to create your own Debt Elimination Plan. I also have developed a tool on the website www.bringoutthemillionaire.com , where you can simply click on Debt Free Drive, enter the debt, interest rates, and balance, and your personalized Debt Elimination Plan will be generated for you. I highly recommend you do this to save yourself time, and to ensure that you develop an accurate plan.

YOUR DEBT ELIMINATION PLAN

Month_____ Year _____

Date	Amount	Creditor	Balance
___/___	$_____	_____	$_____
___/___	$_____	_____	$_____
___/___	$_____	_____	$_____
___/___	$_____	_____	$_____
___/___	$_____	_____	$_____
___/___	$_____	_____	$_____
Total	$_____	Total	$_____

Month_____ Year _____

Date	Amount	Creditor	Balance
___/___	$_____	_____	$_____
___/___	$_____	_____	$_____
___/___	$_____	_____	$_____
___/___	$_____	_____	$_____
___/___	$_____	_____	$_____
___/___	$_____	_____	$_____
Total	$_____	Total	$_____

Month_____ Year _____

Date	Amount	Creditor	Balance
___/___	$_____	_____	$_____
___/___	$_____	_____	$_____
___/___	$_____	_____	$_____
___/___	$_____	_____	$_____
___/___	$_____	_____	$_____
___/___	$_____	_____	$_____
Total	$_____	Total	$_____

Month_____ Year _____

Date	Amount	Creditor	Balance
___/___	$_____	_____	$_____
___/___	$_____	_____	$_____
___/___	$_____	_____	$_____
___/___	$_____	_____	$_____
___/___	$_____	_____	$_____
___/___	$_____	_____	$_____
Total	$_____	Total	$_____

When debt works and when it doesn't

Is there ever an appropriate time where debt is permissible? I personally believe that some debt can be appropriate, especially in the case of purchasing a home, education, and possibly a car. Typically, a home and education are the types of purchases that will yield a good return over the long term. However, even in these instances, I would encourage you to be prayerful about the amount, and whether it is really God's will for you to take loans even for these purposes. If you do feel comfortable with having a mortgage, educational, or car loan, I would encourage you to make a plan to pay those debts off early as well.

If you already own a home or a car, add those balances to your debt elimination plan on the website. You may be shocked at how quickly you can pay off your current balances and be freed up to increase your long-term reserves, and redirect your savings to giving and other long term financial goals you may have established.

Even if you choose not to redirect the money you save once you've paid off any consumer debt to your home or car payments, you can still work on paying off your home or car loan quickly.

Paying your home mortgage loan off early

Whether you have a 15-year or 30-year mortgage, you can pay it off early by participating in a bi-weekly payment program, or by simply establishing an extra amount to pay toward the principal each month or year. Either of these strategies can lead to saving thousands of dollars over the life of the loan.

Take a quick look at the following table. A $100,000, 30-year home loan, with a 7% interest rate and a monthly payment of $665.30 per month, will cost $139,508.90 over the life of the loan. Just paying an extra $100 per month on that same 30-year loan will decrease the interest over the life of the loan to $89,001.74; that's a savings of $50,507.16 over the life of the loan. In addition, instead of taking the original 30 years to pay the loan, paying just an extra $100/month will decrease the time saved to pay the loan off by 9 years and 5 months.

HOME MORTGAGE LOAN REPAYMENT COMPARISON		
	REGULAR PAYMENT	PAYING AN EXTRA $100/MONTH
LOAN	$100,000	$100,000
TERM	30	30
INTEREST RATE	7%	7%
PAYMENT	$665.30	$765.30
Total interest paid over the life of the loan:	$139,508.90	$89,001.74
Actual term of loan	30 years	21 years 7 months
INTEREST SAVED WITH $100 PRE-PAYMENT		$50,507.16
TIME SAVED		9 YEARS AND 5 MONTHS

You can achieve similar results by sending in this extra principal amount on an annual basis. Check with your mortgage company to confirm their policy about accepting additional principal payments, and to confirm whether it needs to be sent in or noted separately. Also, some mortgage companies offer you the ability to participate in a bi-weekly program, where you can make payments every two weeks instead of once a month.

Using the same scenario above, your new payment in a bi-weekly program would be $332.65. Bi-weekly means that you will make payments every two weeks. Over a 12-month period, you will make 26 payments. The two extra payments each year will result in one extra home payment. The interest saved over the life of the loan in this scenario is $34,462.64. Again, check with your mortgage company in advance to see if they offer a bi-weekly program. If not, you can confirm that they allow additional payments, and add the additional amount to your monthly payment.

Either way, you can see that just a little extra money, or simply changing how you pay your home mortgage, can lead to huge savings and reduce the time it takes for you to pay off your home.

Paying off your car loan early

Just like you can pay your home off early, you also can use the same strategies to pay your car note off early. Extra payments or bi-weekly payments can significantly reduce the interest and time it takes to pay off your car. In addition to these methods, however, you might also pay your car note weekly.

I know it seems strange, but paying your car note off weekly can be one of the simplest and effective ways to manage your car payment. Of course, this strategy is most effective if you get paid weekly. We used this strategy to pay off our car early. The weekly payment worked to even out our cash flow, and we paid the car off at least 6 months early.

Paying off student loans early

With the cost of college rising, you or your child may end up with some student loans, even if you have been diligent in saving over the years. Again, extra payments to cover the principal will work just as it did with the car or the home but, with student loans, you might also consider employers who might have programs that repay the student loan based on how long you stay with the company. In some instances, teachers who agree to work in certain school districts, or at certain *at-risk* schools, may be offered student loan reimbursement. Research every opportunity to have these loans paid off, either by a current or future employer. There may be funds or grants available that you are just not aware of.

In addition to employers who might offer tuition reimbursement programs, be sure to do your research on the front end regarding loan programs that might be subsidized by the state. In Texas, for example, students are eligible for a *B On Time* loan. With this type of loan, the loan is forgiven if the student maintains a *B* average and graduates on time. This type of loan is not always available, since it depends on the state to offer it; but if it is available, this can be a great tool for getting a loan, especially if your child is already maintaining good grades and is expected to graduate on time.

The bottom line again for student loan early repayment is to do your homework. Seek guidance from the counselors and financial aid office at your school so that you can be informed of every opportunity to have your loan forgiven or to take advantage of opportunities to apply for scholarships, grants, or other aid.

Establishing Good Credit

Whether you are trying to pay off credit card debt or qualify for a home, establishing a good credit score is important. In general, the better your credit score, the lower your interest rate, payment and, consequently, the overall interest that you pay for something over the life of the loan. Although there are different types of credit scores used for all types of loans, the most commonly used is your FICO score.

While a FICO score of 800-850 is considered exceptional, a score of 670 or higher is considered a good score.

Your first concern is to know what your score is. When you are denied credit, you are entitled to a free credit report from the credit agency that the company used to make the decision. For example, if you were applying for a home loan and were denied, and the bank or mortgage company with which you applied for the loan at used Equifax; then you could obtain a free copy of the credit report from Equifax. In addition, that bank or mortgage company would have to send you a letter to explain the reason why you were turned down.

Review your credit report regularly to dispute any information that is inaccurate. If you do find inaccurate information, it is important to send in the appropriate documents to dispute the information directly to the credit agency. I also suggest that you do the same with all three of the major credit reporting agencies.

In my own experience, I have had major information misreported on my personal credit report that I've had to dispute. Even when I thought it was resolved, I found out a few years later that it was not. So, once you have disputed whatever discrepancy you might have on your credit report, allow a few months for the report to be updated and request a new copy to make sure the information is corrected.

Credit scores don't move quickly, but they can be improved over time. Below are just a few tips that you might take to help improve your credit score over time.

- Pay your bills on time – I know that this may seem obvious, but late payments really drag down your credit score.
- Pay your bills off – Again, obviously, this helps, which is why the debt elimination plan is crucial.
- If you have balances, try to keep them low.
- Try to avoid debt to begin with (let "Don't Even Buy That" be your mantra).
- Consider whether the debt payment will be too much for your current budget.
- Only apply for credit that you need.

This list is not all inclusive of every strategy that you can implement, but I've found if you just at least do the first three things mentioned, your credit score will be headed in the right direction.

At this point in your journey, you've put together a Budget and a Debt Elimination Plan; now it's time to look at some amazing ways to begin creating and protecting generational wealth through your journey on Insurance Lane.

Chapter 5

I could write an entire book just on insurance; but, since I know you are not as excited about Insurance Lane as I am, my objective is not that you know everything about it, but simply that you recognize the need for and importance of it. Insurance, simply put, is the protection of your ASSETS, GOALS, and DREAMS. Car Insurance, for example, protects you against THEFT or DAMAGE to your car. Life insurance protects your family's WAY of LIFE and is one way to create GENERATIONAL WEALTH. How does insurance protect your DREAMS you might ask? Try not having the right type of insurance when life's storms happen, and you will see how everything else that you've learned on this journey to financial freedom can come apart.

Proverbs 13:22 states, "A good man leaves an inheritance for his children's children..."

Proper insurance can help you to leave a financial legacy to the ones you love, and protect the legacy you are building, even while you are alive.

For this part of your journey, I highly recommend you contact a knowledgeable insurance agent in your area and purchase the right amount of insurance for you. If you don't already have an agent, feel free to go to my website, bringoutthemillionaire.com for a list of agents/companies that I feel are especially good with different types of insurance. I'm sharing agents and resources that I know of, but I don't know everybody or everything. These are simply my picks. You might already have a good agent or trusted advisor and, if you do, great! You can simply use some of my references or recommendations to run them by your current agent/advisor or to make comparisons if you are shopping for different financial products.

The next few steps on the journey will give you an overview of the main different types of insurance. Let's start with my favorite: Life Insurance.

Life Insurance—You Know You Gotta' Die

My mom is one of the funniest women I know. She's smart, she's witty, and she has so much common sense. I used to sell life insurance and, when I did, my mom would always say, "I don't see what the big deal is. I don't understand why people don't buy life insurance. After all, *you know you gotta' die!*" I'm laughing even now as I think about the sincere expression on her face as she would say that.

Inevitably, someone—maybe a loved one or close friend—would call and say they needed a donation because a person in their life had just passed away and did not have life insurance. You've been there, right? Well, of course, my mom, being the sweet woman she is, would usually give a donation of some sort, but she would feel bewildered by the fact that they did not have life insurance.

As a former life insurance agent, I discovered five main reasons why you might not have life insurance.

- You don't qualify because of poor health.
- You had it through work and when you left that company, you also left the insurance.
- You don't understand it.
- You procrastinate because you feel nothing will happen to you.
- You can't afford it.

Outside of the very first reason, the remaining reasons, I feel, are simply excuses. Even the first reason may be something that you can turn around if you make some lifestyle changes. Here is my response to each of those reasons for not having life insurance.

- Get healthy (if it's not a terminal illness and you can).
- Get some insurance outside of work.
- Read the Life Insurance 101 section below to get a basic understanding.
- Go to bringoutthemilllionaire.com for a list of agents/companies.
- You can't afford NOT to have it. After all—You Know You Gotta' Die!

Life Insurance 101

Term insurance

There are two basic types of insurance—term insurance and whole life insurance; everything else is simply a hybrid of these two types. Term insurance, as the name implies, covers a person for an indicated term. That term could be 5, 10, 20, or even 30 years. Since the coverage does not last for the person's whole life, it is just temporary insurance. Why have temporary insurance? After all, like my mom said, "You know you gotta' die!" I personally think term insurance has its place. Since it is temporary, you can purchase a larger amount for less money. It is best used to give the person a great amount of coverage when it's most needed.

For example, when my husband Kevin and I first got married, we purchased a 30-year level-term insurance policy. We certainly expected to live past 30 years from the time we got married but, at that time, we had just purchased a new home, were young in our careers, and we wanted to make sure that if either one of us died at an unexpectedly early age, the surviving spouse would be able to pay the house off and comfortably care for our son. Even though we have since moved to Houston, and purchased another home, we are not concerned that the policy period on that 30-year term policy is almost over because, by then, our home would be paid off, and our son would be older and capable of taking care of himself. *(At least that's our prayer—graduate and get a good job, Kirk!!)*

Whole life insurance

Whole life insurance is insurance designed to be around for your whole life, just as the name implies. As you may have guessed by now, whole life insurance is more expensive than term insurance. Scratch that. Whole life insurance usually costs more at the beginning than term insurance. However, in my opinion, because it builds cash value that you can leverage and use for other things, it is a better value over the lifetime of the insured. The way whole life insurance works is that whatever premium you are quoted for coverage, it is guaranteed to never go up. The younger you are, the less the cost of coverage. The older you are, the more expensive the coverage.

When I worked in the insurance industry, I sold both whole life and term insurance. Even though I like whole life insurance for the long-term, some younger couples, starting off in their careers, may not be able to afford the costs of whole life insurance to get the full coverage that I thought they needed, especially if they had young children and had not yet paid off their homes.

I will tell you more about why I like whole life insurance when we get to Saving and Investment Avenue. For now, just know that I don't think it is horrible; some whole life insurance makes good sense as a part of your overall financial plan.

A combination of the two

I've read a lot of books and sat in quite a few financial seminars. There is always this ongoing debate about which insurance is best. Some experts say term insurance is a waste of money because you may not have to make a claim. Personally, I don't think it is a waste of money to have the peace of mind regarding my hopes and dreams for my son's financial future. But, that's just me.

Other experts argue that you should only have term insurance. You should buy term insurance, then invest the difference. I'm a nerd, so I get this—ON PAPER. In the real world, however, most people are not going to take the time to figure out the difference in cost between term insurance and whole life insurance. So, they certainly are not going to invest the difference. If you are the exception, go for it. It works.

When I worked as an insurance agent, I was exposed to a type of policy that combined term and whole life insurance. Kevin and I still had the term policy which would cover our mortgage, but we also purchased a policy that had additional term insurance and some whole life coverage to take care of final expenses in the event of our deaths, no matter what. The other reason I like whole life insurance as a part of the package is because you don't know what life has in store. When you're young, you may think you just need the basic coverage because your house cost this amount, the kids need this amount for college and, by the time you die, or your spouse dies, you won't need that much coverage. Show me one widow, however, who is mad that their spouse left them too much insurance.

To summarize the two basic coverages, I put this chart together for easy comparison. What kind of financial person would I be, after all, if I didn't have at least one chart in the book? NERDS RULE!!! LOL!!!

	TERM	WHOLE LIFE
Premium	Increases after term	Level
Death Benefit	Level	Level
Cash Value	None	Builds
Coverage Period	Typically, 5, 10, or 20 years	Your entire life
Best used for	Covering a mortgage or other loan; a starting place if needed.	Final expenses; leaving an inheritance.
Cost	Premiums lower at first; may become significantly higher after the term specified.	Premiums higher at first, but don't go up.

Health Insurance—YES OBAMACares

Health insurance protects you from EXCESSIVE MEDICAL BILLS and could help you avoid FINANCIAL RUIN.

No matter what your political affiliation, having adequate health insurance coverage is a critical step on your journey to financial freedom. I personally love the intent behind the Affordable Health Care Act. I think that the Democrats have neglected to take control of the conversation regarding the Affordable Health Care Act. Initially, those opposed to the act were quick to associate the Obamacare name as if the whole plan was an abomination. However, I slowly noticed that once its popularity increased, the pundits started calling it the Affordable Health Care Act. I never got around to starting my own personal campaign to print on every bumper sticker and T-shirt I could find, "YES, OBAMA*Cares;*" hence, the name of this section. So, that's my twenty seconds of politics. Now, back to Insurance Lane.

Unlike life insurance where you know that death is coming, you don't really know if a sickness or illness is coming. You don't know when. You don't know how much it will cost but, if you don't have health insurance when you need it, it can not only lead to financial ruin, it may also lead to death.

At the time of this writing, my husband is 44 years young. He has had brain surgery and back surgery. Did we expect that he would have brain surgery? Was it something that we could ignore and hope would go away? Would he be here today if were not for God and the brilliant surgeons who removed his tumor? Would we have been able to get the surgery if we didn't have proper insurance coverage? At the time he had this surgery, fortunately, Kevin was employed full-time with a company that he had worked at for about five years. We had great insurance coverage and, thankfully, could get the surgery done with little out of pocket costs.

A few years later, Kevin was not working full-time with a company. He worked contract, and we had health insurance through the company he was contracting with, however, when that contract ended, so did the health insurance. Due to the previous surgery and other health conditions that we both had, we were turned down for private health insurance and opted to pay for insurance through COBRA. *The Consolidated Omnibus Budget Reconciliation Act (**COBRA**) gives workers and their families who lose their health benefits the right to choose to continue group health benefits provided by their group health plan for limited periods of time under certain circumstances, such as voluntary or involuntary job loss...* https://www.dol.gov/general/topic/health-plans/cobra

Although we were fortunate to have access to this continued coverage, paying for it was no easy task. It was the equivalent of paying two house notes at the time. We paid it.

Then, back surgery. No, we didn't have the low deductible that we had with the company covered health coverage, but I'll take a $2,000 deductible over a $36,000 hospital bill any day.

The sum of it all is this: you need health insurance. You don't know when, if, or how you may have a medical emergency, but the absence of health insurance can lead to possible financial ruin. On the website, www.bringoutthemillionaire.com there are several links on Insurance Lane that can help you find a company or agent to give you more information about the right plan for you.

Home/Auto Insurance—Are you in good hands?

No, I didn't work for Allstate; but my current agent does, and she is a Rockstar!!! Shout out, Ruth Williams!!! If you own a home or a car, you are probably already well versed in home/auto insurance. Just like life insurance protects your life and your legacy, home and auto insurance protect your home and car.

However, some of the coverages protect a lot more than your home and car. For example, your auto insurance can protect your savings if you have sufficient *medical coverage* for yourself, a passenger, or even the driver of another car if you are found at fault for a car accident. Likewise, on your homeowner's policy, you have protections against claims that a visitor may make against you if they are injured on your property.

On your auto policy, you might also have *rental coverage* to cover the cost of a rental car for a short period while your car is being repaired. I personally like the rental reimbursement coverage so that I can be assured that I have transportation while my car is being fixed. The type of coverage that you select will vary depending on your situation and what other insurances you already have in place.

I have adequate health coverage in place, but I still opt for the ***medical coverage*** offered under the auto insurance policy. I do this mostly because the world has become a very sue–happy place. Even when the other driver tells you it is okay, and they are okay, it is amazing how once they get home and start adding up the dollar signs, their stories change. So, for my peace of mind, I keep the medical coverage in place.

This sue-happy environment that we live in might be another reason that you consider **Umbrella Insurance**. Although this type of coverage is usually a separate policy from your homeowners and auto insurance, it picks up where they leave off. If you don't have significant assets, this may not be a coverage you choose to have. However, if you are a business owner and have significant assets, check with your agent to determine if this type of policy would be appropriate for your situation.

Another factor that you should be aware of is that your credit score may affect your auto and homeowner's insurance rate. Yet another reason to pay special attention on Debt Free Drive.

The key advice that I have regarding homeowner's and auto insurance, outside of just making sure you have it, is to review your coverage options and compare rates at least once a year. Ask your agent about any possible discount, even if there may be one that you did not previously qualify for. If you have a great agent, they will usually send out a review reminder annually. This is also a great time to compare the rate they are offering to another company's rates.

You've probably seen the word *agent,* and a good company, more on Insurance Lane than you will in any other place on your journey to financial freedom. I believe in having an accountability partner in this stage of your journey to financial freedom because there is so much that you may not know. The role of a good agent, whether it's life insurance, homeowner, auto, disability, or long-term care, is to educate you about your options and hold you accountable to implementing and sticking with your plan.

Sure, you may be able to find a cheaper rate with an online company but, in most of the insurance areas, I find that a good agent pays for themselves. I won't give additional dialogue about disability insurance or long-term care insurance here. I've just created a checklist with the various types of insurances so that you can quickly review the list to determine if you have them. Once you go through the list, if there is one you are not sure about, feel free to go to www.bringoutthemillionaire.com to find an agent in your area.

INSURANCE CHECKLIST

Health Insurance (Circle One)

1. Do you have this kind of insurance?	Yes	No	Unsure
2. Do you feel that it is adequate?	Yes	No	Unsure
3. Do you need more information?	Yes	No	Unsure

Car Insurance (Circle One)

1. Do you have this kind of insurance?	Yes	No	Unsure
2. Do you feel that it is adequate?	Yes	No	Unsure
3. Do you need more information?	Yes	No	Unsure

Disability Insurance (Circle One)

1. Do you have this kind of insurance?	Yes	No	Unsure
2. Do you feel that it is adequate?	Yes	No	Unsure
3. Do you need more information?	Yes	No	Unsure

Long-Term Care Insurance (Circle One)

1. Do you have this kind of insurance?	Yes	No	Unsure
2. Do you feel that it is adequate?	Yes	No	Unsure
3. Do you need more information?	Yes	No	Unsure

Homeowner's/Renter's Insurance (Circle One)

1. Do you have this kind of insurance?	Yes	No	Unsure
2. Do you feel that it is adequate?	Yes	No	Unsure
3. Do you need more information?	Yes	No	Unsure

Life Insurance (Circle One)

1. Do you have this kind of insurance?	Yes	No	Unsure
2. Do you feel that it is adequate?	Yes	No	Unsure
3. Do you need more information?	Yes	No	Unsure

At the funeral

Do you know if he had life insurance? I'm not sure; I know he did when he worked at the Railroad.

I don't think he had it because I overheard them talking about taking up a collection to cover the funeral expenses, and they're taking him to the country because they already have a plot there.

Do you know if she was saved? I really don't know. I mean she used to go to church with us all the time when we were younger, but she's had been out of church for a while now and I had not heard her mention anything about God or Jesus recently.

Question: Why do you wait until the person is dead to ask whether they have life insurance? Don't answer that. I really do get it. It's a funeral. Of course you want to know; especially if it is someone that is close to you. But is it going to make a difference at this point? They can't come back from the dead and purchase a policy. It's too late, which is why I think this question should come up while the person is living.

The funeral expenses will get taken care of, eventually. However, there is one type of insurance that I intentionally left off my initial Insurance Checklist above which can save a lot of people from asking the second question AT THE FUNERAL.

INSURANCE CHECKLIST
(cont.)

Eternal Life Insurance

1. Do you have this kind of insurance?	Yes	No	Unsure
2. Do you feel that it is adequate?	Yes	No	Unsure
3. Do you need more information?	Yes	No	Unsure

Eternal Life Insurance

In my opinion, this is the most important type of insurance that you can have. It doesn't cost you a dime, and it leaves a priceless legacy to your children and their children. This type of insurance is the kind that comes from praying the simple prayer of salvation as follows:

Lord Jesus, please come into my life. I know that I am a sinner. I repent of my sins. I believe that

*... **You are the son of God***
*... **You died on the cross for my sins***
*... **You rose again so that I may have eternal life***

AMEN

I know I talk a lot in this book about creating generational wealth and leaving a legacy, but I must say that the best inheritance that I have received from my family is the spiritual inheritance that has come from me accepting Christ at a very young age. I was raised with an awareness that there is a power greater than me at work. As I grew older, I saw tangible ways where God's favor allowed me to afford and be a part of things that my family could not write a check for (or, just didn't have to write a check for).

I will tell anyone who will listen that my mom has so much favor. I know it is because of her faith. I always say that I want to be just like her when I grow up. It's not just because of her wit and humor, and her love of life; it is because of the *faith walk* that I've seen her have for the 45 years of my life.

If you don't have a relationship with God, please consider reflecting on the Eternal Life Insurance offer above. And, guess what, I have the references and resources for help with that on my website too!!! Just go to www.bringoutthemillionaire.com and click on Eternal Life Insurance; you will see a link to resources and, in some cases, churches in your area that can help you to grow in your relationship with Christ.

Chapter 6

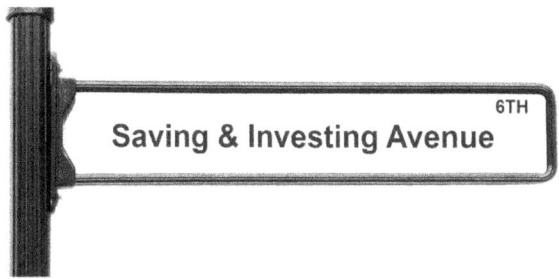

My Lawd will save me

("My Lawd" is "My Lord" as spoken with a sweet distinguished southern twang.)

If you have accepted the Eternal Life Insurance offer on Insurance Lane, you are now a Christian. As a Christian, depend upon God to save you. And He will. But I am often reminded of the story about the man that was in the flood, who was depending upon God to save him too. The waters were rising; someone came by on a jet ski and offered to take him to dry land. "That's alright," the man replied. "My Lawd will save me."

Then, the waters kept rising. By this time, the man was sitting on the kitchen counter top. His neighbors came by in a boat and begged him to go with them. But he was standing his ground. "You go ahead," he told them. "My Lawd will save me."

Well, after some hours had passed, the man had to make his way to the roof of his house. A helicopter came by and sent down a ladder for the man to grab and climb up. "I'm okay," the man screamed from the roof top. "My Lawd will save me!"

Sure enough, the man drowns, dies, and goes to heaven. While he is excited to know that he made it to heaven, he is a little upset that his Lawd didn't save him. He approaches the pearly gates. "Lawd," he asks, "Why didn't you save me?" God replies, "*Well, I sent the jet ski, the boat, and the helicopter. Why didn't you use it?*"

I feel God is asking you the same question: "Why didn't you use it?" I sent you down Budget Boardwalk so you could figure out where your money is going. I told you, DEBT—Don't Even Buy That. Make your debt list; create a debt elimination plan. But you had your debts under control. I even told you to "Bring Out the Millionaire in you," but you told me that what you're doing was already working for you. "Why didn't you use it?"

Now, put together a plan for your savings because, right now, your savings are saving you. You have it at the bank, but you need it away from the bank—somewhere you can't touch it. You use it when you need a new outfit, but you should be using it only if you have no outfits at all. You let it accumulate with no purpose and no target. Even I know that the disability insurance doesn't kick in for 90 days—you should have at least three months of income as your goal.

My Lawd will save me! Act like you want to be saved.

Put it on Automatic

Contrary to popular belief, you DON'T have to be rich to save and invest. The most important components to saving and investing are DISCIPLINE (having a plan and sticking to it) and DIVERSIFICATION (not putting all your eggs in one basket). For many, AUTOMATIC SCHEDULED DRAFTS (from your paycheck or bank account) offer the most effective ways to CONSISTENTLY save a lot of money over a long period of time.

"The wise man saves for the future, but the foolish man spends whatever he gets." (Proverbs 21:20)

The quote from Proverbs above says a foolish man spends whatever he gets. The most effective way that I have found to save over the long term is to not allow yourself to *get* the money you plan to save in the first place. AUTOMATIC SCHEDULED DRAFTS from your bank account or your paycheck directly into a savings account, preferably not at the bank you have your regular checking at, can be a powerful way to build savings over the short and long-term.

I'm not anymore disciplined than you. I have goals and dreams just like you. I have things that can break my budget if I'm not careful. So, I take the same measures that I am telling you to be successful at building a sufficient savings.

Short-term savings

Now, we do have a savings account at our bank, but that is not our *true savings* account. It was simply opened, I think, to avoid a monthly fee at the bank. We fund it with very little each month and use it as a slush fund when we get off track with our budget, or if we have an unexpected expense occur that isn't in our normal monthly budget.

For short-term goals that are coming up within the next year or so, we use an online banking account. Although this money is not drafted directly from our paychecks, we have AUTOMATIC SCHEDULED DRAFTS that are deducted from our account when our paychecks hit the bank. **FORCED DISCIPLINE**. We like to travel. This, for us, is not an optional expense in our budget. So, we plan for it. Even if we are not sure exactly where we are going, we know that we will get a call, usually from my sister-in-law Andetria (who is the family's bootleg travel agent), telling us when, where, and how much it is going to cost. So, we plan for it out of every check.

Maybe it is not travel for you. It may be shopping or fixing your house, or decorating. Whatever the goal, if you're serious about saving for it, open an account away from your regular bank, decide how much you can afford, and start your **AUTOMATIC SCHEDULED DRAFTS.**

Why an online bank?

Thank you for asking. If you have a bank that is only online, it typically takes 1-2 business days for the money to be transferred to your regular checking account. This helps you to avoid using this money that you have tagged for a certain savings goal to fund any short-term or impulsive spending decisions. It keeps this savings from SAVING you.

Long- term savings

Remember back on Insurance Lane when I told you I really liked whole life insurance? This is another reason why. *You know you gotta die, right?* But you also need to build up a long-term reserve of 3 to 6 months of your salary in case of an emergency. I like whole life insurance because it offers you a vehicle to do both at the same time. There is nothing fancy about it; the interest rates are not spectacular, but you do earn interest on a consistent basis, typically more than you can earn in a money market, CD, or other bank offered instruments. Now, to be fair, most of those things that you get at the bank are going to be FDIC insured, and you don't get that insurance when you purchase whole life insurance; but, if you choose a good company, your savings should be safe.

I also have peace of mind that if I really needed to access funds, I can take a loan against my insurance policy. Then, when I paid the loan back, my cash value would be restored. Yes, I would be paying interest back to the insurance company when I repay the loan, but I am also paying myself back, since paying back the loan helps to restore and enhance the cash value of my policy.

If you are not eligible for insurance, using an online banking account works for your long-term savings as well. However, I would suggest considering even a 3rd banking institution, so your long-term savings doesn't get mixed in with your short-term savings.

Investing 101

"Give portions to seven, yes to eight, for you do not know what disaster may come upon the land." (Ecclesiastes 11:2)

Who knew that the Bible had so much wisdom in it surrounding investing? This verse in Ecclesiastes is the cornerstone for most successful investment plans—DIVERSIFICATION. This is the perfect time for me to quickly explain Stocks, Bonds, and Mutual Funds.

Stocks

Do you have a car? Who made it? Did you buy anything today? What store? That company very likely offers stock that you can purchase. When you purchase a share of a company's stock, you are purchasing a small piece of that company. When that company does well, the value of your stock goes up; when that company doesn't do well, the value of your stock goes down.

Bonds

When you purchase bonds, you are financing a company, municipality, or government's debt. For example, if a city needs to build a new highway, they may issue bonds to sell that will finance the cost of that project. The bonds are backed by the city or entity issuing them. You, as the investor, purchase the bond. The city agrees on a certain percentage rate to pay for that bond, and you earn the interest on that bond for the stated time period. When the time period is up, you receive back the initial investment.

Mutual FUNds

Unless you have a lot of time on your hands and a lot of money to invest at once, it can be challenging to build a well-diversified portfolio of stocks and bonds simply by purchasing one share at time. Mutual FUNds are designed to let the average investor be a part of the market without having to invest a lot of money at once, or without having to be knowledgeable about every single company they own.

So, with a mutual fund, you can invest as little as $50/month, in most cases; instead of buying a share in 1 company, you buy a small share of every company that is within that mutual fund. Now, when that mutual fund does well, so does the value of your share and, when it goes down, same thing.

Most mutual funds are professionally managed by people who do nothing all day but watch the market and research different companies that should be in that particular mutual fund. When you invest in a professionally managed fund, you pay a sales charge and fees. That's right—people actually do not work for free. You do have to pay to invest. However, if you are working with an advisor to choose the right funds for you, over time, that advisors fee will pay for itself.

Index Funds

I do have to mention that there are other mutual funds that simply follow the indexes. You may have heard of the S&P 500 Index, for example. A mutual fund that is modeled after the S&P 500 Index will have companies in it that are in the S&P 500. So, the returns on the fund will be similar to the returns that are experienced by that index. These funds are *passively* managed. Since the managers are not actively selecting the companies inside the fund, these index funds can usually be purchased without an upfront sales charge; although most of these funds do still have fees.

The Umbrellas

Now that you have a basic understanding of Stocks, Bonds, and Mutual Funds, it's time to look at the Umbrellas—at least that is what I call them.

You've heard the names of the umbrellas—401ks, Roth IRA's, Traditional IRAs, 529 Plans.

I consider taxes *rain on your financial parade*. I call these different vehicles *umbrellas* because each of them offer some type of tax benefit or protection to whatever investment you place under it.

Come back Angie!

I hear you.

It's time for a CHART. Don't judge me; I like them.

Take a look at the chart on the next page. Across the top are some of the different *umbrellas*. The rows represent the money at different stages of the investment. Essentially, these umbrellas will stop or minimize the *rain* or taxes at some point in the cycle.

For example, if you save money in your 401k through work, you will usually get to deduct whatever money you put in from your taxable income immediately. So, you are using pre-tax money to invest. When the money you invested grows, you won't have to pay taxes on the earnings. The 401k *umbrella* loses some of its coverage when you take the money out because that is when you pay taxes on the earnings.

By contrast, if you invest in a Roth IRA, the money you put in is not tax deductible. However, it does grow tax-free and, when you take it out, it comes out tax-free. There are additional guidelines for these umbrellas and other umbrellas but, hopefully, this gives you a better understanding of some of the more common ones.

THE UMBRELLAS				
	401K	Traditional IRA	Roth IRA	529 Plans
MONEY YOU PUT IN	Tax deductible	Tax deductible	Not tax deductible	Not tax deductible
EARNINGS	Tax free	Tax free	Tax free	Tax free
MONEY YOU TAKE OUT	Taxable	Taxable	Tax free after age 59 1/2	Tax free if used for qualified college expenses

On Insurance Lane, I recommended you have an agent to help you fully understand the different nuisances of insurance. Here on Saving & Investing Avenue, I strongly advise you to work with a financial planner. Sure, continue to learn about different saving and investment vehicles on your own, but I have found that working with a good planner will help you be accountable for your goals, and he or she can continue to educate you as you grow and learn.

Rule of 72—I Ain't Mad At Ya

I can't stand my sister! Don't get me wrong. I love her to death. I'm a true little sister. If she says the sky is blue, then it's blue. If she says I need to have balance, I seek it. If she tells me that outfit looks good, I walk with an extra bounce in my step. I respect her opinion. I love her, but sometimes I just can't stand her, and the story I'm about to share represents one of those times.

Years ago, I told her I was talking to the Marriage Ministry at our church about the *Millionaire in You*. She said, "I already know there is a millionaire in me. Yeah, yeah, yeah... The Holy Spirit lives in me. God owns everything. I'm his child. So, I'm a millionaire too. Now, BRING IT OUT!!!!!" I wanted to slap her. And I wanted to slap her hard! (Of course she was right, but I didn't appreciate having to go back to the drawing board to make this clear.)

The best way I can write this story is to just repeat the conversation I had with my sister. The italicized parts are my sister's comments. The other comments are my own.

Okay, so I show up at my sister's door on Wednesday, September 17, 2003, with all of my books, notes, and guides so we could talk through this series.

Deb:
Okay, Angie. The Millionaire in You is a good course, but you never really told me how to become a millionaire on paper. Show me the money.

Me:
Deb, that wasn't the intent, totally. The intent was to make people understand...

Deb:
Yeah, yeah, yeah. I get that. And I ain't mad at ya. But, we already know that. How do I become one on paper? You said you were going to tell me how to do both—discover the millionaire in me and become one on paper. Remember? And you said you were not going to wait until the last class to do so. Now, tell me.

Me:
Okay, you missed that class. That was Savings & Investments Avenue. I talked about mutual funds. I brought different things from the pantry at home. I explained how we don't have to just be consumers of Heinz ketchup, for instance; we can own the company. I explained mutual funds and the Rule of 72, and how compound interest is the 8th wonder of the world.

Deb:
Okay. That sounds good. Explain it to me.

Me:
Okay. The Rule of 72 says that if you earn, say 8%, on a $1,000 investment, well, you simply divide 72 by 8. That's how long it will take for that $1,000 to double—9 years.

She just looks at me.

Deb:
Girl, tell me, how I can become a millionaire?

Me:
I grab my financial calculator. $1,000,000 Future Value. 6% APR, $800/month, solve for Years. Thirty!!! (She won't go for that, I think. So, I keep punching in my calculator. Okay. Okay, what about 8%? 28 years.)

Okay, Deb, if you invest $800 dollars monthly, and get an 8% return, then by age 70 you will have a million dollars.

Deb:
Okay. Okay. But, I'm 42. What if I only did $600/monthly until I was 65? How much would I have?

Me:
About $473,000.

Deb:
So, you're telling me if I invested $600/ monthly, for23 years, I'd have roughly $500,000.

Me:
Yes.

Deb:
I ain't mad at you!!! Okay, now what if I bump that up to $800/monthly.

Me:
Well, that would be about $630,000.

Deb:
I still ain't mad at you!!! You have told me if I invest $800/monthly, for 23 years, by 65 I'm going to have over a half a million dollars.

Me:
Yes, but remember this is hypothetical. Instead of 8%, you may earn 5%. Or even -5%, -10%, or -20%. But, yes, if all those variables played out, yes. You see, here is what happens.

I'm thinking about using this in my presentation. I show her *Taking Turns at the Top Sheet* . Okay. Most people invest this way. Follow the gold square that says Large Cap Stocks.

Deb:
Okay.

Me:
Let's say you started investing in 1997. You see that Large Cap stocks were up, so you bought them. Then, the next year, they went down. So, what did you do?

Deb:
I sold them.

Me:
Right. But the next year they went up again. So, you buy them here when they are at the top. Let me ask you something. How do you make money investing? Do you buy high, sell low, or buy low, sell high?

Deb:
Buy low. Sell high.

Me:
Right.

But that's not what most investors do. So, what we suggest instead of trying to pick the right fund or the right time to invest, is have a little bit of all of these asset classes and smooth out your ride over the long term.

Deb:
Okay. That chart is okay. But only spend about 30 seconds on it. Like you did just now. Now, back to this.
(pointing to my calculator)
You have already told me that if I keep going until I'm 70, I'm going to have a million dollars, right?

Me:
Right.

Deb:
Okay. Now, you also have some insurance money for me too, right?

Me:
Yes, right now you have mostly term insurance. Do you remember when I explained that? Term insurance is like renting an apartment. Permanent insurance is like buying a home. Well, you, and most of my young family couples need so much insurance with the kids, the mortgage, etc. that you have mostly term insurance. But each year, I'm having you change a little bit of that to permanent so you will have some cash value to supplement that retirement money.

Deb:
Okay. How much money would I have from my life insurance at age 65?

Me:
500K

Deb:
Oh, I'm really not mad at ya!

Me:
Oh, Deb, I'm sorry; that is age 85. Age 65, well, that's about 120K.

Deb:
Humph. Okay, I'm okay.

Me:
She is looking a little like "I'm not mad at you; I just don't like you as much."

Deb:
But, okay, that 500K that I have for retirement—how much interest can I draw from that half a million?

Me:
Well, we would suggest you draw no more than 5% annually. So, about $25,000 a year.

Deb:
How much is that monthly?

Me:
About $2,000.

Deb:
Hell, I Ain't Mad At You!!! You have all this money coming out of my account anyway. I don't even miss it. You could be taking $800 a month right now, and I wouldn't know it.

Me:
Yes, that's the power of AUTOMATIC SCHEDULED DRAFTS.

Deb:
I know. Now, tell them that in class. Tell them how much they need. Then, send them a card. Okay, you need to put away this amount to get there. How much do you want to start with?

Me:
Deb, that's what I do. I start my clients somewhere. I try to get them into the 10% mindset. Then, when I have their annual review, we enhance it.

Deb:
Yep, that is what you do. Write that down. Now, that's a class. I Ain't Mad At Ya!

Me:
Okay.

Deb:
But, now I would be mad at you if you had not made me do anything to build a solid financial house. But, really—I Ain't Mad At Ya!

The early bird gets the worm, but the late bird can still eat

In most financial books, this is where you will get the chart that shows you what could happen if you invest a certain amount of dollars at age 25 and then stop, and let it grow for 40 years. Then, the comparison is to what happens if you wait until you are 40 years old to start investing. I was guilty of showing this comparison to my clients as well.

I have to say, though, even though the early bird gets the worm, the late bird can still eat. There are more worms!! It is not too late to start investing. It is not too late to start BACK investing if you got off track. So what if you're older; you are probably making more money and can afford to tuck more away. You can waste time being regretful about what you haven't done or you can commit to start TODAY. If you noticed back on Budget Boardwalk, when I listed the categories, I placed Savings and Investing right under Giving/Tithes. I DID THAT ON PURPOSE.

If you haven't yet read the book *Rich Dad, Poor Dad,* by Robert Kiyosaki, buy it and read it today. I read this book in my mid-twenties and it confirmed some of the philosophies that I had toward saving. Read it for yourself, but here is my take away. Poor Dad: pays for everything else first; then, if there is money left, saves and invests for the future. Rich Dad: saves and invests first, and then pays for everything else.

THERE WILL ALWAYS BE SOMETHING—SOME BILL. SOME EMERGENCY. SOMETHING.

Saving and investing must become a priority. If you are strangled by the Masters on Debt Free Drive, I beg you to set yourself free. Do the work that you need to do to get out of debt. But start saving now!

My mom reminded me of how I used to save my pennies when I was a little girl so that I could buy Christmas presents for my family. Pennies add up to nickels, dimes, quarters, and dollars.

Maybe for you it's not saving pennies; it might be picking up cans and selling them. Maybe it is taking on an extra job, just until you get the debt cleared out. Whatever you must do to start saving, please do so. Make saving a priority.

Your Personalized Investment Plan

Investing with a goal in mind is like going on a journey. You should know where you are trying to go and when you are planning to get there. With today's smartphones, we use GPS systems to guide us wherever we want to go. We just put in where we are and where we want to go, and we let Siri (team I-Phone) take us from there.

On my website, www.bringoutthemillionaire.com I have some GPS systems in place for you. Whether your journey is to obtain $1,000,000 by the time you retire, or $50,000 to pay for your child's college, you need a personalized investment plan. Simply click on the link for Saving & Investment Avenue, and you will be able to open calculators for retirement or college planning.

These calculators are great for planning a perfect trip, with no traffic and no detours. In financial language, that means that these calculators provide hypotheticals only. You put in your answers to a few questions, and the calculator will generate a scenario based on you earning a certain interest rate every year without fluctuations. Whether you earn that annual rate will depend on the returns of the actual investments you choose. However, it will at least give you an idea of what you need to do to reach your goal.

Go ahead and plug in your millionaire goal. You might be shocked at the amount you need to put aside to reach it. It may be less than you anticipated, especially if you are younger, or even if you're not. It may be higher but, if you start somewhere, you will at least have more than you had if you don't do anything, right?

So, I encourage you to use the tools to finish mapping out your personalized investment plan.

Now, there is one more place that I want you to travel on your way to Millionaire's Row. This next stop is where you will learn how to build your REAL Estate and enhance your investment plan through home ownership and, possibly, investing in real estate.

Chapter 7

*H*ome Ownership: *One of your best Investments*

When I was in school, I noticed that a lot of my classmates wore the latest and greatest fashions, but when I visited where they lived, it didn't match my expectations. I'm not saying they lived in shacks; I mean that most of them lived in an apartment instead of a home like I did. I didn't get it. They had designer jeans and shirts, and the latest edition of Jordans. Why didn't they live in a house like mine? Now, mind you, I didn't grow up living in a mansion, but it was a nice home. Later, I realized that some people who I thought were buying their homes, had been renting. In some cases, these individuals had been lifetime renters.

Why?

Home ownership had not been a priority for them. I am so glad that it was important to my parents and that they instilled this type of desire in me. My dad and I were talking the other day, and he said, "Real estate will always sell because they're not making any more of it." It's not the first time I heard this, and he's not the first person I heard say it, but it bears repeating here.

Owning a home is a great investment, especially if you know that you are going to be in one place for a significant period. You are going to have to pay to live somewhere anyway; why not own it? I saved Real Estate Parkway for one of the last stops because you will need to have some money saved up to invest in real estate, whether it is your primary home or a rental property. So, when you are starting off on your journey, you should make saving for the down payment on a home a part of your long-term savings plan.

I suggest saving at least 20% for a down payment; however, you may be able to purchase a home with as little as 10% down. Either way, you need funds for the down payment.

Finding the right realtor

Once you have the funds for a down payment, you need to find a good realtor. Once again, I was very fortunate because I have a Rockstar real estate agent, Patricia Berholtz, with Remax. Shout out, Patricia!!! The best way I can sum up what to look for in a great real estate agent is to sum up how Patricia worked for me.

- She was prepared.
- She listened.
- She showed me homes in my price range.
- She educated me about the process.
- She had her own Rockstar team to walk me through the mortgage loan process.
- She negotiated a great price for me.

When I purchased my first home, I was young and straight out of college. I was very fortunate because I had a very generous brother who loved his family, and I had money saved up to put money down on a home. But I was moving to Atlanta, and I didn't really know the area, so I got a referral from one of my brother's friends who lived there. Patricia met me, my Mom, and my sister shortly after we arrived and, within a few days, she helped us find the perfect townhome in a great location for a great price.

Fast forward, 3 years later—Kevin and I were planning to get married. So, we were buying a bigger home. Since the original home I had purchased had appreciated in value, I was able to use the money from the sale of the first home to put a down payment on the second home, which Patricia found for us. We repeated this process when we moved to Houston.

The initial money that I invested in my townhome in Georgia was probably around $15,000. Just looking at that initial investment, it has grown and doubled at least twice when I consider the equity in my primary residence today. So, stocks and bonds are great, but if you are going to pay to sleep somewhere anyway, why not let it earn money for you over the long term, and help you along your journey to financial freedom.

The mortgage loan process

Although purchasing a home is exciting, going through the mortgage loan process is not. Yes, I have a superstar Realtor. She has superstar mortgage loan officers that I've worked with over the years, but the process is still tedious. In addition to making sure that your credit is in good condition so that you can qualify for the best possible rate, there are lots of documents that you have to be prepared to share with the mortgage company or bank when applying for a loan.

Here is an abbreviated list of the things that you typically need to be underwritten for a home loan:

- Your Tax Returns for the last two years
- Two to three months of your most recent bank and retirement statements
- Two years worth of W-2s or 1099s if you are self-employed/independent contractor
- Your most recent paystubs covering one to two months

Then, once the lender has run your credit (and questioned you about the unreturned library book that you forgot to take back when you were 6), you get offered different rates and scenarios for loans.

You pick a loan and rate that you are comfortable with. You schedule a closing. You get a HUD settlement statement before closing so that you can review where every penny of the money from the loan will be spent and, if needed, you bring a cashier's check to cover any expenses that are not covered by the lender, seller, or by the loan itself if you have it structured that way.

The closing itself is pretty painless (except that you have to sign a million papers and you feel like you are signing your life away without knowing it).

I know I am making this process seem so painstaking but, the first time I went through it, it really wasn't that bad. I think it really was because I was working with Patricia's Rockstar team. By the second home purchase, I knew what to expect, but since that was the first home Kevin and I purchased together, the paperwork was more intense.

No matter how painstaking the process, though, the results are worth the effort. For the investment of time and energy that it takes to get qualified for the loan, the home purchase is worth the effort of getting your records to the mortgage company and going through the approval process.

In case you skipped Debt Free Drive because you don't have any consumer debt, I want to reiterate that even though you may choose to get a mortgage to purchase your home, you should consider accelerating your mortgage loan payoff so that you can free up that money to fund your other financial goals. Please review that section so that you can make a goal to pay your home off early.

Rental property

I like investing in real estate through purchasing a primary residence, but I also think it is a wise to own investment property as well. Investing in a second home is a lot simpler if you already own a home. I still recommend a good real estate agent, but I also encourage you to invest in educating yourself about real estate investing in your area.

You may consider joining a real estate investment club, or you might even just find a mentor who is already investing so that you can learn the ins and outs of investing in your local market from someone who is doing it already. Real estate investing is a great way to further diversify your investment portfolio.

You purchase an undervalued home and make the investment to fix it. Then, you can either resell the home for an immediate profit or choose to rent it out for the long term, allowing the renter to pay for the home over time. Once the home, or homes, that you have chosen to invest in are paid off, you have now created additional sources of income that you can use to supplement your retirement.

If you talk to a real estate investor, they will tell you real estate is the only way to invest. If you talk to a stock broker or financial advisor, they may tell you that mutual funds are the only way to invest. They are both wrong. Do both. Why not?

It may take a while before you have the assets to invest in a home or additional real estate properties, so invest through your company's 401k, or open a Roth IRA and invest in mutual funds in the meantime. Either way, do your homework and know what you are investing in. Get some counsel from an advisor, agent, or mentor who is doing what you are interested in, and who is knowledgeable about the type of investments that you are considering making.

Chapter 8

Over the next few weeks, months, and years, if you implement the practical strategies outlined in this book, you will *Bring Out The Millionaire In You.* I hope that you will enjoy the journey and, hopefully, establish that you are already a millionaire by your relationship with God.

Here on Millionaire's Row, I thought it would be great to share just a few success stories of some of my past clients who have already discovered they are millionaires by their relationship with God and who have or are well on their way to becoming millionaires on paper as well.

Millionaire by Relationship—My Mom

I know I mention my family a lot in this book, but I must take this time to tell you a portion of my Mom's story. I've shared that I am the youngest of five children and that my mom was a single mother from the time that I was 12. What I want to share is how my mom's investments in her faith and in her family paid off for her over time. My mom worked as a beautician for over 20 years. She didn't make a lot of money, but she was always great with managing her money. I remember watching her put money in an empty butter container every month to save for her annual vacation. Yes, even as a single parent of five children, she made time for herself to take a vacation. She didn't really learn about investing in the stock market until I became a financial planner years later, but she did know about investing her time and energy into her family. It paid great dividends. My mom is the epitome of a Proverbs 31 woman. We, my siblings and I, call her blessed! My brother, Craig (Rodney), always talked about having money and allowing my mom to retire; when he became a professional football player, he did just that.

So, you do the math. How could a single mom of five children afford to retire at age 50? I told you, according to the federal poverty levels at the time, we were poor. It's because she made good investments in her family and our activities—little league games, cheerleading, basketball, football, academics, student council, etc. She made sure she gave us a spiritual inheritance by sharing God with us at an early age and keeping us in church. My mom continues to live a blessed life. Craig retired her, and she has made some wise investments to take care of her basic needs. My siblings and I have helped to continue to supply her with just a little more of her wants. She received good returns—good fruit is what I call it.

Millionaires on their journey to becoming Millionaires on Paper

As I was wrapping up this book, I asked some of my former clients who are on their way to becoming *Millionaires on Paper* to share just a few of their testimonials about how this work, which I have had them do over the years, has impacted their lives. Here are just a few of their comments:

You taught us the importance of planning for the future. You supplied us with the knowledge and importance of different types of insurance and investments. Even though we didn't always use everything you told us as planned, it truly came in handy when we needed it—even today, nearly 20 years later. You taught us to trust the information and to do something. And, oh yes, sorry about riding up on a motorcycle for our appointment to increase our life insurance. – Debbie

I really value your lessons on couples working together financially. – Reginald

Angie was young and got my attention that I needed a plan for 30 years later when I retired. I am so glad she woke me up to start investing and to get a plan started. Today, I am a few years from retiring and have the nest in which this bird can relax and enjoy one of my favorite investments—my condo that views the blue ocean in Puerto Rico, where I can watch the whales passing by. I only wish I had known Angie before I was in my forties. Her persistence and follow up let me know she believed in her program and cared about me. – Patricia

Working with Angie, I learned to be cognizant of the real value of the money you budget and save over time for a goal. For me, this translated into the funds I was putting away for my kids' college fund. I was very proud of starting early and saving $100/month. Angie sat me down and asked me what my goal was for this money and made it CRYSTAL CLEAR that at the rate I was saving, I had enough money for 1 semester of junior college. It surprised me, but it helped me to realign my expectations for the real cost of college, and I increased my savings immediately. – Cheryl

We always thought about life insurance as an unnecessary expense. Angie explained why some types of insurance was important to have to provide for loved ones in the event of an unforeseen loss. While our coverage amounts have changed over time, thanks to Angie, we still have some form of life insurances to this day! – Alan and Thuy

Angie helped us to start on a retirement plan through investments and life insurance, and she encouraged us to save money for college for both of our sons. They have now both graduated and we were able to offset some of the cost of college with the savings that Angie encouraged us to start when the boys were young. – Randy

Your journey

I wanted to share the testimonials above because they are from real people who have real situations, and they have taken real steps towards their journeys to financial freedom. I must take the time now to remind you, however, that this is still YOUR JOURNEY. I hope that you have learned some things as you went down Stewardship Street, Budget Boardwalk, and Debt Free Drive. But faith, without works, is dead. It's time for the rubber to meet the road. Get in your car and drive through this journey—Your Journey to financial freedom.

If you really take the time to read the testimonials, you will notice that they are not perfect. No one's journey is perfect. You will have some detours. You might be "under construction" on some parts of your journey for a while. Know that it is okay. It's just like the GPS system on your phone or in your car. If you get off course, what does Siri say? Re-routing, re-routing.

The important thing is to keep going or, if you must stop and get some directions because Siri decided to go on break, pull over and ask for help.

Let me know where you are on your journey

I don't know everything; I'm still learning on my journey too. But I hope you can take at least one, two, or three good ideas and implement them so that you can *Bring Out the Millionaire in You.* Please email me and share where you are on your journey. I would love to hear about your success, and maybe even some of your not so pleasant experiences, so that I can continue to learn through your experiences as well.

Let me know how I can help

If you would like help in going through your journey, remember to go to the website, www.bringoutthemillionaire.com. There is a wealth of resources and websites to help further educate you. Also, if you want more one-on-one coaching, or would like information about an upcoming live webinar or seminar, join the mailing list and I will keep you posted.

Thank you for allowing me to share what God has placed in my heart regarding the biblical principles and financial strategies for you to BRING OUT THE MILLIONAIRE IN YOU.

ACKNOWLEDGEMENTS

God, thank you for birthing this idea in me, over 20 years ago, and for giving me the wisdom to know then that I didn't yet know enough to write the book and that the book would write me.

Kevin, my husband, thank you for living out this journey with me. I love you so much. I am excited to see what God will have us do next.

Kirk, my son and creative genius, thanks for your input in this process. Now, get back to the books.

Mom, you're the REAL MVP! Most of the lessons I have learned about money, and especially about budgeting, came from watching you work magic with the funds you had while we were growing up.

Dad, because you were such a great provider, I grew up with a Millionaire's Mindset. Thank you.

Deb, my coach, sister, and friend. Thanks for pushing me to get this done. You know it would not have happened without you. I'm so proud of the work you did with your book, Giving Birth to Your Home-Based Business. You truly live out how to grow your business and still have time for yourself, family and friends.

Kelvin, Randy, and Craig—you're the best big brothers a girl could have. Thanks for your support and help in getting this book done and getting the word out.

Kim "Possible" Porter—Because you did, I knew I would have to. Your book, *The Assignment*, is still my go-to when I need to get my life back on track. Thank you.

A special thanks to family and friends that helped with proofing & editing: Cheryl Fisher, Gregory Ficklin, Carolyn Ficklin, Andetria Hampton, Monica Hampton, PhD, Stacie Hampton, Sandra *Favorite Cousin* Love, Debbie Porter, Kim Porter, and Pamela Prevo. Your feedback was so helpful in fine-tuning this work. Thank you so much!

To all my family and friends, whether you realize it or not, you played a role in this book. There are too many of you to list, but you know who you are—THANK YOU and I LOVE YOU DEARLY.

Raymond Aaron, you made writing this first book so simple with your 10-10-10 program. I am so glad I showed up that rainy fall day in Houston. The team you have put together to hold my hand throughout this process has been amazing. Cara Witvoet, my personal book architect, thanks for holding me accountable to my deadlines and for the feedback each step of the way. Lisa Browning, my editor, thanks for catching all the "little things" that make such a BIG DIFFERENCE. Waqas (bookcoverartist.com) thank you for reading my mind and notes to come up with the perfect cover.

A special thanks to my *A Better Bail Bond* family. We have the keys to everyone's freedom from jail. This book has the keys to everyone's financial freedom.

To my favorite School of Business professor at Howard University, Dr. Philip Fanara, thanks for challenging me to learn the numbers behind the numbers.

To my spiritual teachers, both those who have gone on and those still living, who have poured into me from a young age. **The late and greats**: Rev. William Mayes, Sis. Annie Driver, Sis. Shirley Ellison, and

Rev. Leonard Driver (Solid Rock Baptist Church). ***The greats:*** Dr. Ross Cullins (Solid Rock Baptist Church, Houston, TX), Rev. Kenneth Stewart (Solid Rock Baptist Church), Rev. Vernon Hubbard (Connecting Fellowship Church, Houston, TX), Rev. McCallister Hollins (Former pastor Ben Hill United Methodist Church, Atlanta, GA), and Dr. Ralph West (The Church Without Walls, Houston, TX). The wisdom and faith that I have gained under your teaching has helped to shape me into the woman I am today. Thank you.

To Howard Dayton and the late Larry Burkett, thank you for the Crown Ministries Bible Study. This financial bible study helped me gain a new perspective on how God intended for me to the handle money, time, and talents that He has blessed me with. Linda Pitts, Anita Hill, Linda Edwards, Wendell Johnson, Larry Johnson, and the other members of Ben Hill's Financial Literacy team from 1998, this book is, in part, the result of the lessons I learned through our shared experiences and through the workshops and seminars we put on together. Thank you.

Mentors: To Cassius Williams and Sam Bridgeman (previous Managers during my New York Life Insurance days) -- you are the type of Hidden Figures that movies will be made about 20-30 years from now. Thanks for all of the mentoring that you shared during my time with you. George Frye, thanks for expanding my knowledge of the mortgage business and giving me insight on the bigger picture of financial planning.

Finally, to my mentors who don't even know they mentored me: Oprah Winfrey, thanks for the *edu*tainment through your show and now through your network. Steve Harvey, you are a bootleg preacher. Thanks for your humor and inspiration. Joel Olsteen and family, thanks for the reminders to have faith and stay positive in every assignment God gives us. Suze Orman, thanks for making the conversation about money a common topic of conversation, and for inspiring me to do what you have already done. Kirbyjon Caldwell, your book, *The Gospel of Good Success,* provided a pivotal moment for me in my twenties by teaching me that God wants us to prosper and have good success. Les Brown, I knew there was greatness in me; thanks for the reminders over the years.

ABOUT THE AUTHOR

Angela has spent over twenty years working with individuals and businesses in financial planning, helping them to get their finances in order. From college and retirement planning for individuals to business succession planning for small businesses, Angela has lived out her mission of teaching biblical principles and financial strategies to individuals and businesses so they can build a solid financial house. Angela has a vision for financially free families to create generational wealth, invest in God's kingdom, and live out the wisdom of Proverbs 13:22—"A Good man leaves an inheritance to his children's children." This book outlines the strategies for you to do so.

Angela is a proud Howard University School of Business Alum, and shares this honor with her husband, Kevin. They have one son, Kirkland, who is currently completing his undergraduate studies at Howard University as well. Angela lives in Houston, TX and is currently a member of The Church Without Walls in Houston, TX where Dr. Ralph West is the Pastor.

www.ingramcontent.com/pod-product-compliance
Lightning Source LLC
Chambersburg PA
CBHW071208220526
45468CB00002B/548